Discipleship By Design

The Discipling of Christian University Students

Harvey A. Herman

xulon PRESS

Discipleship By Design
by Harvey A. Herman

Printed in the United States of America

ISBN 978-1-60647-644-4

www.xulonpress.com

Dedication

To my wife, Sally, who introduced me to university student ministry

To my daughter, Sarah, her husband Rob, and to my son, Matt, with his bride Tracy who are discipling students at the University of Aberdeen, Scotland and at Cornell University

Faithful and fruitful disciplers, each and every one of you

You are the joy of my life

Table of Contents

Acknowledgements

It was March 1977 at a national campus minister's conference. I met Brady Bobbink for the first time. Brady described how he was implementing discipleship at Western Washington University. A few years earlier I had been deeply challenged by Robert E. Coleman's book, *The Master Plan of Evangelism.* Brady was implementing Coleman's principles with secular college students. Coleman's principles and Brady's implementation came together for me. I am indebted to Brady's teaching and his model of campus ministry. His ideas are woven throughout this book.

I have been greatly influenced by Dr. James Bradford, David Argue, the training materials of Chuck Miller, and Lyman Coleman. Special recognition must go to the thousands of students who are living out the principles described in this book. And thanks to the scores of campus minister's who have offered encouraging feedback throughout the years.

Thanks to Matt Myers for the superb cartoons. Thanks to Calvary Chapel of Seattle for providing a writing sabbatical to finish this project.

The following publications granted permission for the original publication in 1991:

Unless otherwise noted Scriptures references are taken from the *Holy Bible, New International Version.* Copyright 1973, 1978, 1984 International Bible Society. Used by permission of Zondervan Bible Publishers.

"Keys Ingredients for Community," Lesson 1. Adapted from *Covenant to Care*, Louis H. Evans, Jr. Victor Books. Used by permission.

"Human Resources Specialist," Lesson 2. Source Unknown.

"Young Communist Letter," Billy Graham Association. Lesson 3. Used by permission.

"ACTS Prayer Format," Lesson 10. Source Unknown.

"Deeds of the Flesh," chart. Lesson 11. Source Unknown.

Preface

Discipleship By Design was originally published as a manual in a three-ring binder in 1991. Over the past seventeen years a host of university ministers and church pastors report it is an effective tool for training discipleship leaders for campus small groups and church cell groups. It is now translated into several languages including Spanish, French, Russian, Polish, and Arabic.

In the original preface I said, "The intent of this manual is to assist the campus pastor to pursue the ideals expressed in the Chi Alpha philosophy of ministry. The manual's goal is to place a philosophy of discipleship in the hands of the campus pastor. It provides a tool to assist in the discipling process."

This book like the original provides a seven-chapter section that lays a framework or theology of discipleship. The *Discipleship Framework* examines the discipling method of Jesus and unpacks principles such as: "disciple the faithful and pastor the unfaithful."

Following the *Framework* is a twelve-lesson series of *Student Lessons* to be used in a seminar or classroom setting. The first four chapters of the *Discipleship Framework* and the first six lessons of the *Student Lessons* focus on the theological and philosophical foundations for the discipling process. The remainder of the *Framework* and *Lessons* unpack the implementation of these foundations. The book follows a pattern employed by the apostle Paul when he penned several of his epistles. He first addresses, "Who you are" before going on to "What we should do." This book is similarly organized to deal with the "why" of discipleship before dealing with the "how". The *Framework* is written with the pastor in mind, while the *Lessons* are written with the university student in mind.

Though written for a campus ministry context, *Discipleship By Design* may be very beneficial for the training of home group leaders in a local church. Many churches simply translate the campus ministry illustrations into local church situations.

How To Use This Book

Discipleship By Design (DbyD) began as a student leadership-training manual written by a campus pastor and used effectively for several years with secular college students. As other campus pastors heard about DbyD, they asked for the manual to be edited for their benefit. As such, all the illustrations and language reflect the secular campus ministry environment.

Nevertheless, a local church pastor will quickly recognize a comparable context and easily apply these principles into his/her local church. I found lay leaders in my church easily understood the principles and instinctively knew how to apply them.

The purpose of *Discipleship By Design* is to assist the campus minister with discipleship training in the university setting. It is designed to equip disciple-makers. It trains your leaders in the theological foundations and practics of small group discipleship. Then it goes beyond that to equip your people in one-to-one discipleship. As such, it is an excellent means to assist with the training of discipleship small group leaders in a campus ministry, or the home cell group leaders of a local church. It equips your people in the process of making disciples.

The book is divided into two distinct sections. A Discipleship Framework is a seven-chapter section directed at the campus minister or church pastor. It deals with a biblical and philosophical rationale for discipleship, and provides practical guidelines on how to develop a discipling campus ministry or local church. The Discipleship Framework is best used in a leadership retreat where the goal is to design your organizational blueprint to developing disciples. It will help frame your planning and discussions.

Part Two: The Student Lessons is a twelve-lesson class with the student or lay leader in mind. They originally served as the class notes for a 12-week, 90-minute class on the discipling process. It is more effective to use the Student Lessons as the foundation for discussion rather than as follow-along material for a class lecture. As such, in many cases no teacher is required. Frequently, students will sit and read the lesson together and discuss what they are reading at their own pace. An instructor who is able to lead class discussions will find this material very helpful.

I suggest several different and effective approaches to using DbyD:

1) Establish a 60-90 minute class that meets weekly for twelve weeks. This could be a late afternoon class on campus, or it's been very effective as a Christian education class in a local church.
2) Since student schedules are so demanding, try using two consecutive Saturdays for six hours each. In an abbreviated manner cover the content from Student Lessons 1-6 on the first Saturday and 7-12 on the second Saturday. Many campus groups are presently using a variation of this idea.
3) If you already have small groups established in your campus group or church, use the Student Lessons as the content of the small groups for a quarter.
4) Blend content from both the Discipleship Framework and the Student Lessons into your existing training program for leadership development. Many groups have taken this approach, especially drawing primarily from the Student Lessons 7-12. This blends the leadership principles crucial to your situation with small group dynamics and equips your people with practical training in small group and one-to-one discipleship.
5) Have students read the book as a self-study project. After they have read DbyD and Robert Coleman's *The Mater Plan of Evangelism* sponsor a weekend retreat to discuss what

they read and determine how you will implement the information into your campus group or church.

Discipleship By Design is not intended to be the final word on the discipling process by any stretch of the imagination. Rather, my prayer is that it assists you to be more effective at fulfilling the Great Commission to "disciple the nations."

Part One

A Framework for Discipleship

Foundations and Practices of Discipleship

"As Jesus walked beside the Sea of Galilee, he saw Simon and his brother Andrew casting a net into the lake, for they were fishermen. 'Come, follow me,' Jesus said, 'and I will make you fishers of men.' At once they left their nets and followed him." Mark 1:16-18

The relationship between Jesus and these two brothers started with the simple words, "Come, follow me." In essence, a disciple of Jesus is a follower. Jesus' twelve followers eventually will change the world. This is an inconspicuous and unremarkable beginning for an eventual team of world-changers, don't you think?

After the resurrection and just before Jesus ascends into heaven he intently looks his followers in the eyes and commissions them to go everywhere in the world and repeat the process of making disciples. The inconspicuous beginning results in an unfathomable assignment for a motley collection of young men who had never ventured more than a few dozen miles from their birthplaces. Simply, how can this happen? How will an assortment of "unschooled, ordinary men" (Acts 4:13) be transformed into courageous and substantive heralds in just three short years?

Transformation, complete and deep-seated transformation, is the answer. How does a metamorphosis of the life happen in a new follower?

Clearly education is part of the process, but certainly not all of it. As I review the many discipleship programs I've seen, and the books I have read, you would think education is the full answer. Right thinking is assumed to bring the inner transformation of the heart and soul. If this were true, one could assume Christians in America would be the most robust believers ever to walk the planet. Christians are regularly taught from pulpits and podcasts and from a plethora of books and TV preachers. A follower can pick from scores of different Bible translations. If education is the answer to transformational followership, then why are so many believers so ambiguous in their beliefs and behaviors? Why is church membership in decline?

Discipleship for Jesus began with relationship and an invitation to join a missional community. Before followership is a program it is experienced in a culture. The next seven chapters initiate a dialogue on how to foster a culture of discipleship. Before discipleship is programmed it must be processed. No program can fulfill The Great Commission. However, a community of believers committed to transforming the world through the process of making disciples can.

Chapter 1

A Foundation for Discipleship

Why Disciple Students?

Any society that seeks to map out a road to a better future must plan a trip through the university campus. The time a student spends in college is filled with dreaming dreams and seeing visions. Students don't just envision a better tomorrow. They also develop into the very agents of change that transform the future. The great universities of America are leadership factories producing leaders for every sector of our society. It is crucial then for Christians to take a sober look at the campus, when they set plans to advance the kingdom of God on earth.

Therefore, the proclamation of the gospel of Jesus on campus is critical. This student generation needs Jesus as Lord of their lives. We shudder within when we consider a world led by people nurtured upon the worldview surrounding today's student. If we fail to respond to the desperate need of today's university student, the church shall reap a whirlwind of apocalyptic trouble, and these students will remain enslaved in their sin.

The action needed is not only an unapologetic and convincing proclamation, but an adamant adherence to the primary injunction of the Great Commission to "make disciples of all nations." Every nation of the world can be found on the American university. Every nation can be reached by investing time and energy on the campus.

Not only do students need new life, they must be shown how to live that new life. They must be discipled. I cannot imagine a more strategic and potentially powerful disciple of Jesus Christ than the American collegian.

Jesus' goal in the discipling process is fruit bearing. It is wonderful to see a new branch grafted into the Vine. How much better to see those grafted into Jesus bearing spiritual fruit. "This is to my Father's glory, that you bear much fruit, showing yourselves to be my disciples" (John 15:8).

If the new life from the gospel is to remain visible and active, then deliberate and purposeful discipleship must occur on the campus. Most of today's students are far afield from a Christian worldview. With our help they must come to understand the kingdom of God, accept it, grow in it and know how to reproduce it in others.

Many believers, unfortunately, share the common experience of never having been deliberately or purposefully discipled themselves. It is one thing to call strongly for discipleship. It is another thing to know what discipleship entails and how to participate in the discipling process. If we have never been personally discipled ourselves, we will be unsure as to how to disciple another. Therein lies the purpose of this book. In this chapter I suggest six essentials of the discipling process.

Godly Character Shapes a Community

Our world is facing a leadership crisis. We see the crisis in the political arena, in the sports world, the military and, tragically among church leadership. The crisis reflects both a lack of character and the necessary leadership skills.

The good news of the gospel addresses this crisis as it involves a transformation of believers into new creatures in Christ Jesus. This inner transformation is a central issue in the discipleship process. A true disciple of Jesus is characterized by the fruit of the Spirit and by a desire for holy living and integrity. A disciple is one who is spiritually enabled to walk the talk.

Yet, growing up into the image of Christ does not happen in a vacuum. Being righteous before God is a relational issue. You cannot sin unless you transgress some relationship, be it either with God or another person.

Stated more positively, living a righteous life will manifest itself in our relationships. It is impossible to disciple aside from the community of God's people. One-on-none discipleship does not exist. Growing in Jesus demands our full participation in the life of the body of Christ.

What should the "abundant life" look like between members of the church? Should they not be honest and forgiving, also respectful and peaceable? They must speak the truth (even sometimes when the truth may not be popular) in love (even when love may not be felt).

Disciples are affirming people. They look to see all the potential and possibilities that Jesus sees in another person and sincerely affirm them in their brothers and sisters. Disciples are open and vulnerable people who don't hide their true inner selves. Disciples risk and trust because Jesus did. Disciples seek to know another while at the same time seeking to be known.

Therefore, one of the essentials of the discipleship process is that it occurs in a relational context. Just as Jesus chose twelve men "that they might be with him", so discipleship must occur in fellowship where believers can be known and be able to know others well. Solomon stated this principle well, "As iron sharpens iron, so one man sharpens another" (Proverbs 27:17). By clearly focusing on discipleship, a local community of believers is transformed corporately as well as individually.

A Global Vision Launches the Mission

Jesus tells his disciples they will become his witnesses in Jerusalem, and eventually to the ends of the earth. To Jesus discipleship did not hinder the evangelization of the world, but discipleship was in fact the means to evangelize the world. Jesus came to reach the world with good news with saving, healing power. He did so by discipling twelve men in the message and method of the Kingdom of God. The point here is simple, but is often missed. Jesus intended to reach the world, and he accomplished his goal through discipleship. For us, any goal less than world impact is too small a goal. Discipleship is Jesus' method to reach his goal. If we are faithful to disciple in our Jerusalem, the message and power of God's salvation will go around the world.

Where more unquestionably could this occur than on the universities of our world? One man who saw this clearly and exhibited a worldwide vision was Charles Habib Malik, past president of the General Assembly of the United Nations. Listen to his words, "The university is a clear-cut fulcrum with which to move the world. The problem here is for the church to realize that no greater service can it render both itself and the cause of the gospel, with which it is entrusted, than to try to recapture the universities for Christ.... More potently than by any other means, change the university and you change the world."

The Chi Alpha Campus Ministries' philosophy of ministry confidently believes that if you reach students for Christ, you will transform the university, the marketplace and the world. It places its primary focus upon the community of Christ becoming all it can be. The community on campus is to express itself in intercessory prayer, worship to God, fellowship with one another, witness to the lost, and discipleship at every level of relationship in the community. For discipleship to become truly effective, the community must embrace its incredible potential. A lifetime of faithfully discipling a few at a time will, in fact, have a global impact.

A Compassionate Response to Human Need

Poverty, ignorance, alienation, disease, hostility, greed — the list could go on. Jesus is the answer! Each one of these aberrations from God's design for humanity breaks his heart. What do they do to our heart? It is true that the problems of the world seem overwhelming. The desire to insulate one's self from the problems is a very human tendency. Nevertheless, when we position ourselves in isolation, unmoved and untouched by the needs around us, this strips Christ from Christianity.

What motivates a discipler? Compassion, the kind only Jesus has and only he can give. A discipler who lacks a pastoral heart that can be touched by human longings can be dangerous. To be entrusted with the words of life and then treat them as some kind of new law to enforce upon others does grievous harm to the cause of Christ.

Scripture tells us "love covers a multitude of sins". Experience tells us that love covers a multitude of ineptness, as well. A discipler who truly cares and shows it will be responded to in like manner. Love that is patient, kind, trusts and hopes is God's love. As Paul says, "Love never fails." We should have as a motivation the pursuit of effectiveness in ministry. But effectiveness in ministry skills without a real expression of love is very confusing and can be damaging.

A Theology Forged from a Sound Hermeneutic

Discipleship must stay on track. Our sideboards are *Christ the living word* and the *Bible the written word.* We must learn how to hear both properly. We cannot focus one over the other, for the illumination of the Spirit assists us in understanding the Scripture, and the Scripture guides us in interpreting the Spirit's communication to us.

One of the most essential skills we must learn and then teach as disciplers is how to study the Scriptures inductively. God's Word is our authority for all faith, belief and practice. We must learn how to feed ourselves and then show others how to feed themselves upon God's Word. We must disciple in such a way that people maintain their dependence upon Christ alone. It is improper to create a dependence upon the discipler to the degree that the protégé gives away the responsibility over the decisions that affect his life. A discipler must equip fellow believers to "stand firm...with the belt of truth buckled around your waist."

The discipler must, as well, pray that he will grow in spiritual discernment and in the ability to judge prophetic words. The risen Lord still desires to speak to us today. The Spirit stills wants to address the specific situations in our life, and we must have a firm grasp of Scripture and spiritual discernment to stay on track. Thus, attention must be given to learning proper Biblical interpretation skills while our ear is tuned to hear the voice of the Lord. These must be pursued together without elevating one over the other.

A Commitment Conveyed through Godly Zeal

An indispensable ingredient to discipleship is commitment. Someone has compared the lack of commitment to that of a slipping clutch on a car. The driver has years of experience, the car is well tuned and powerful, the road is smooth; but the clutch will not engage.

It can be the same in discipling relationships. The discipler can be well trained and all parties can have good, warm Christian hearts; but without commitment, the discipling process will fail. Commitment must be taught, expected and modeled.

I have one note of caution here. Commitment for the sake of commitment alone can become quite tedious. This occurs when we focus on the ministry program to the detriment of the people. Jesus called his disciples to incredible commitment. However, it was not to a great cause alone. He called them into relationship with the Father and with himself, and to do the works of the Father. A person doing the works of the Father is filled with godly zeal. That person burns to fulfill God's will. Godly people become committed people who will last.

It was the zeal for the Lord that motivated Jehu to destroy the idolatrous dynasty of Ahab. May we be able to say as Jehu, "Come with me and see my zeal for the Lord" (2 Kings 10:16). Commitment without zeal can be drudgery, and zeal without commitment can be toxic. But commitment that is fed by a zeal for God is powerful in the discipling process.

Ministry Skills that are Transgenerational

To this point in talking about the essentials of discipleship we have identified character, vision, heart and zeal. All of these reflect the inner quality of the Christian discipler. Too often these are overlooked while focusing on the abilities and skills a disciple may display. The leader in the workplace is often made the leader in the church. It's often a good choice but sometimes a terrible mistake. Jesus tells us not to watch what goes into a person but what comes out from that person. The issue of the essential character of the discipler is primary. That is why it has received so much focus.

But that is not to say that ministry skills are unimportant. On the contrary, ineptness is neither a virtue nor any type of blessing. Love may be able to cover it, but it can't hide it. A discipler must make a commitment to grow in effectiveness in the Lord's work.

Some of the skills we will look at later in the manual include Bible study, prayer, needs assessment, goal setting, time management, and spiritual disciplines. The goal of a discipler is to teach these and other ministry skills in a transgenerational manner.

Have you ever had someone tell you, "I know how to do that, but I don't think I could tell you how to do it?" This is true for so many people. They can be great achievers, but they don't have the slightest idea how to tell others how they do it. We must invest as much time in thinking through how we do ministry as we do in actually ministering.

Transgenerational ministry skills are skills that come with instruction manual attached. Not only should I tell you how much you need to study the Bible, but I must have a method to help you get started. And beyond that, the method I teach you needs to be one that you can easily teach another. If I can help you in understanding Scripture and at the same time do so in a manner that equips you to teach another, I have in effect discipled someone a generation removed from me - thus a transgenerational ministry skill. We must teach not only what needs to be known, but also how to know it. It is the goal of this manual to assist you in the development of transgenerational discipleship.

These six goals mentioned present the scope of this manual. It intends to highlight the major issues in campus discipleship. Our hope is that it will assist you in more capably fulfilling the Great Commission to "disciple the nations" in your specific university setting.

Chapter 2

Discipleship and the Jesus Model

The process of discipleship was not new to the Jewish world of Jesus' day. Jewish rabbis had disciples for quite some time before Jesus' arrival. But the manner by which Jesus discipled was radically different. The rabbis bound their disciples to the Torah, the Jewish Bible, and to the tradition of previous rabbis. Jesus bound his disciples to Himself. Jesus required His disciples to surrender without reservation to Him and to the Kingdom of God that he was inaugurating. The Twelve were not official brass following their governor. Being a disciple of Jesus meant nothing less than complete personal commitment to Jesus. And being committed to Jesus included being committed to His message of the Kingdom of God and His method of bringing in that Kingdom.

The Master's Message

Mark in his gospel summarizes in one short verse the entire message of Jesus. Mark records that after John the Baptist was imprisoned and prior to Jesus calling His first disciple, that Jesus was preaching, "The time has come. The kingdom of God is near. Repent and believe the good news!" Mark 1:15.

Jesus came declaring that God's Kingdom was now present and active among His people. This Kingdom was not geographical, but refers to God's rule and reign in the earth. Jesus had come from God to establish God's reign. There were three primary evidences in

Jesus' ministry that exposed God's rule. First, the relationship with God is now one of child-to-Father. Second, the evil spirits that held people in bondage were cast out. And lastly, the sick were healed. These evidences demonstrated the integrity of Jesus' message. Jesus further stated that the Kingdom of God is expressed in two great moments: the fulfillment within history in the person of Jesus, and the consummation at the end of history that Jesus ushers in at His second return.

This is how the parables are to be understood. In the parable of the four soils, Jesus tells us the Kingdom is working quietly, even secretly among men. It is not forced upon anyone, however it must be received willingly. But wherever it is received, it brings forth much fruit. For now, the emphasis is not on the harvest but upon the central act of sowing.

From the parable of the mustard seed, Jesus instructs His disciples that the reign of God will one day be like a great tree and rule the whole world, but until then it appears small and insignificant but it grows quietly. The parables of the treasure and pearl remind us that the Kingdom of God is of inestimable value to be sought beyond all other possessions. If it costs a man everything he has, that is too small a price to pay in return for gaining the Kingdom.

Thus, Jesus taught us discipleship is not merely following a messiah, but to be a disciple one must participate fully in the life of the Kingdom of God. Discipleship is not just learning. It goes beyond that to experience and involvement. It is personal, it is real, it is now, and it is ours to receive. A disciple does not merely recite the teachings of Jesus and thus become mature. A disciple lives out the truth of Jesus' teaching and thus becomes effective with an imperishable agenda to accomplish.

So much more could be said of Jesus' message. And it regularly is being said Sunday after Sunday in the local church. Rightly so, believers have focused on the words of Jesus, for truly they are "words of life". But does the strength of the church highlight at the same time its weakness? We so want to be true to Jesus' teachings, and we must. But do we with equal zeal desire to live as Jesus lived? Do we desire to do the works of the Kingdom as well? There is equally as much to learn by following Jesus' method for world conquest.

Jesus lived with purpose. The way Jesus lived is just as instructive as His words. Jesus expected his hand-picked disciples to live as He lived and do the same works.

The Master's Method

Since it was first published in 1963, Robert E. Coleman's short book, *The Master Plan of Evangelism* has become a classic in its own time. Be careful when you read it! It is easy to understand, but its message is demanding. It demands a life-altering response. Jesus' ultimate purpose is world evangelism, and His method for accomplishing such was through discipleship. Please hear Coleman state the objective of the Messiah in this somewhat lengthy quotation:

> The days of His flesh were but the unfolding in time of the plan of God from the beginning. It was always before His mind. He intended to save out of the world a people for Himself and to build a church of the Spirit which would never perish. He had His sights on the day His Kingdom would come in glory and in power. This world was His by creation, but He did not seek to make it His permanent abiding place. His mansions were in the sky. He was going to prepare a place for His people that had foundations eternal in the heavens.
>
> No one was excluded from His gracious purpose. His love was universal. Make no mistake about it. He was "the Savior of the world" (John 4:42). God wanted all men to be saved and to come to a knowledge of the truth. To that end Jesus gave Himself to provide a salvation from all sin for all men. In that He died for one, He died for all. Contrary to our superficial thinking, there never was a distinction in His mind between home and foreign missions. To Jesus it was all world evangelism.
>
> His life was ordered by His objective. Everything He did and said was a part of the whole pattern. It had significance because it contributed to the ultimate purpose of His life in redeeming the world for God. This was the motivating vision governing His behavior. His steps were ordered by

> it. Mark it well. Not for one moment did Jesus lose sight of His goal.
>
> That is why it is so important to observe the way Jesus maneuvered to achieve His objective. The Master disclosed God's strategy of world conquest. He had confidence in the future precisely because He lived according to that plan in the present. There was nothing haphazard about His life - no wasted energy, not an idle word. He was on business for God (Luke 2:49). He lived, He died, and He rose again according to schedule. Like a general plotting His course of battle, the Son of God calculated to win. He could not afford to take a chance. Weighing every alternative and variable factor in human experience, He conceived a plan that would not fail. (*The Master Plan of Evangelism*, Robert E. Coleman, Revell: Old Tappan, New Jersey, 1963. Pages 17-18.)

It was the purpose of Jesus to reach the world with the good news that God loves, forgives and reigns. Jesus cares about each individual. He provided a salvation for "whosoever will". But His method was not in mass evangelism. Men were His method. The world is not changed by bigger and better ideologies or through highly efficient programs. Jesus set out to change the world by changing men and that in small handfuls of them at a time.

You must understand that this is far more than introducing a person to God the Father, having them confess their sins, and the insisting they attend church. Jesus' method of discipleship presupposes that His followers live in communities of committed relationship with one another. Pivotal to Jesus' discipling is the establishment of community. Jesus committed Himself to building the first Christian community. He carefully selected the first members. Community is not something that is created when people gather together, however. Community is a way of life that transcends mere association and friendliness.

People gather together all the time. They join lodges, neighborhood associations, charitable organizations, virtual communities and so on. But the community of God is very different. It is more than Christians associating together, much more. The discipling method of Jesus demonstrates how Christians are to live with one another. Rather than joining a Christian organization that has programs designed for the public welfare, the challenge for today's church is to live with one another in dynamic relationship sharing the Lord and initiating Jesus. Community is costly, often today's church life is not.

Before Jesus ever performed His first miracle, Jesus picked men. Then He stayed with them. In fact, as the cross loomed closer and closer, Jesus increased His time with the Twelve. The way to reach the multitudes was not by exclusive ministry to the multitudes, but in building men who could reach the multitudes. These men Jesus chose learned to reach the multitudes after Jesus' example, one handful at a time. They were to disciple men just as they had been discipled by Jesus. And they were only successful when their disciples were discipling others.

Being a disciple of Jesus meant carrying your own cross. It meant total commitment to Jesus and His mission. Being Jesus' disciple meant giving yourself away unselfishly, loving as Jesus had loved them. Jesus showed them how to understand the Word of God. He taught them how to pray. He gave them assignments in ministry and then reviewed their ministry upon completion. He held them accountable for what they were learning and the responsibilities He had given them. Jesus worked with them until they began to produce fruit in keeping with their ministry. And then even after they had been discipled, He promised that He would never leave them as they carried out the Father's will.

Community is the foundation for growing in the love and life of God. This foundation is the essential core of Chi Alpha's philosophy of ministry on the secular campus. Our philosophy statement says it well:

> Our primary strategy is to work toward the building of a group or community of people who share the ideals of becoming a community of worship, a community of fellowship, a community of discipleship, a community of mission, and a community of prayer. We believe the most fertile atmosphere for people to come to faith and maturity

in Christ is warm exposure to a group of people fervently committed to the God of the Bible, to one another, and to the task of evangelizing the campus. As a worshipping, loving, discipling, witnessing, praying community, they demonstrate the Kingdom of God and most effectively enculturate others in it.

For effective use of this manual and the class notes that follow, it is necessary that you carefully read Coleman's book. It is used as the background material for lessons 1-4 in the class notes, as well as being the required reading for the class. It carefully explains in 125 pages what can only be highlighted in a few paragraphs here. It illustrates Christian lifestyle and deprograms typical church life. Take great care in understanding the various components in Jesus' discipling method described there. Let it speak to your heart and then to your life. It may call for some changes in your philosophy of ministry. Test it against the Word of God, and then determine to live under the authority of the Word.

Discipleship and The Great Commission

Listen closely to Jesus' final instructions as recorded by Matthew. "All authority in heaven and on earth has been given to me. Therefore go and make disciples of all nations, baptizing them in the name of the Father and of the Son and of the Holy Spirit, and teaching them to obey everything I have commanded you. And surely I am with you always, to the very end of the age" (Matthew 28:18-20).

When this is read in English, the primary impact Jesus intended is often missed. But the intent is quite clear in the original language of the New Testament. Greek is a language of action. In the primary sentence that begins with "Therefore go....", you will find one main verb and several other verb forms. The main verb is amplified by the other verb forms, and the main verb clearly identifies the action to be taken. The main verb is, "make disciples". "Disciples" is actually a part of the Greek word itself.

In Matthew's account he places these words of Jesus as the final conclusion. They are the final instructions from the Lord to His disciples. Like a final will and testament, they are intended by their placement to carry great significance. After all that Jesus had taught them and done among them for over three years, these were His departing words, His Great Commission.

Often it has been said that the focus of Jesus' final words were to "go"- implying that fulfilling the will of God is primarily involved in going. Others have focused on "teaching", while still others on "obedience to everything Jesus commanded". The main verb of the sentence, however, is "make disciples". All the other verb forms augment or amplify the process of making disciples. To enlarge upon the Commission sounds like this: In your going, make disciples - make disciples by baptizing and by sound teaching which leads to obedience to Jesus' commands. The passage seems to indicate that the going, the baptizing, and the teaching should all lead to the goal of making a disciple.

We often think of the will of God as having to do with where we are. We assume that some place is more suited for us to serve God over all other places. But the impact of the Great Commission seems to emphasize that God's will is more concerned with what we do than where we live. You cannot serve Christ everywhere at once, but wherever you are you can make disciples. True, God does call us at times to specific places, but that is only the beginning of fulfilling His will. Jesus would ask, "Are you making disciples where I placed you?"

Discipleship then is central to Jesus' great purpose for His church. The "doing" of our lives must revolve around the discipling process - being discipled and discipling others. It is to be our investment for a lifetime. How are we to invest the talents that the Master entrusts into our care until He returns? We know that we are surely not to hide them, but the investment that brings the greatest returns in the Kingdom of God is to use these talents to disciple. This is real treasure that may be laid up in heaven. Discipleship is a ministry given to us by Jesus that has eternal impact.

Chapter 3

Discipleship as a Way of life

Discipleship, like evangelism, is a biblical mandate. Neither is optional in the believer's life. While many Christians are tempted at times to put on special outreaches and "do evangelism" in an effort to ease their consciences as it pertains to spreading the good news, most know that being a witness is an around-the-clock job in which they are never off duty.

The same could be said of discipleship. For the Christian, discipling should be a way of life - an every moment adventure. Discipleship cannot be approached as a new area of personal growth that one emphasizes for a season. It is not an elective or an add-on to a ministry program. Being a disciple and discipling others is at the very heart of the New Testament definition of effective Christian life. We have already seen discipleship is at the core of Jesus' Great Commission to His church. Rather than an item on the periphery, discipleship is a central issue; a point from which Christian beliefs and lifestyle originate and develop.

Discipleship is Costly

In Mark 1:17, Jesus engages Peter while he is at work and says to him, "Come, follow me." For Peter, following meant leaving behind family, vocation and home. Jesus told Peter at the outset that He would train him for a new kind of fishing, but to learn he would have to leave everything behind. A few years later Jesus comes again to Peter while he is fishing. The last recorded words of Jesus to Peter are the same as the first, "You must follow me" (John 21:22). Discipleship for Jesus' disciples was, and is, very costly.

The cost of discipleship is the call to follow. To follow Jesus is never an achievement or a reward for some merit in the disciple. Rather, it is a first act of obedience to the divine command uttered to all Christians. Peter discovered his calling was a supreme act of grace on God's part. Dietrich Bonhoeffer reminds us, "Such grace is costly because it calls us to follow, and it is grace because it calls us to follow Jesus Christ. It is costly because it cost a man his life, and it is grace because it gives a man the only true life. It is costly because it condemns sin, and grace because it justifies the sinner. Above all, it is costly because it cost God the life of his Son, and what has cost God much cannot be cheap for us. Above all, it is grace because God did not reckon his Son too dear a price to pay for our life, but delivered him up for us." (*The Cost of Discipleship* Dietrich Bonhoeffer, Macmillan: Revised edition, 1959, p. 47-8.) Being a disciple of Jesus is an act of willfully carrying out His wishes, not only a confession of allegiance.

Though costly, responding to the call of discipleship should also be characterized by great joy. Jesus taught, "Again, the kingdom of heaven is like a merchant looking for fine pearls. When he found one of great value, he went away and sold everything he had and bought it" (Matthew 13:45,46). Once we recognize the magnitude of Jesus' offer, we eagerly lay aside all to follow Him. The apostle Paul affirms this, "But whatever was to my profit I now consider loss for the sake of Christ. What is more, I consider everything a loss compared to the surpassing greatness of knowing Christ Jesus my Lord, for whose sake I have lost all things" (Philippians 3:7,8).

If being a disciple is costly, so also is being a discipler. The discipling process demands self-sacrifice, for Jesus demands all our personal resources be made available. A discipler is often open to criticism. Discipling others can wear you out. For this reason it is essential the discipler have a broad biblical foundation for discipleship. When fatigue is overwhelming, the discipler who doesn't fully understand his call may wilt under the pressure.

Perhaps the most disturbing words from Jesus concerning costly discipleship are recorded in Mark 8:34, "If anyone would come after me, he must deny himself and take up his cross and follow me." This cross consists not simply of burdens we must carry. The cross of Jesus certainly didn't. The cross for Jesus was an appalling instrument of death. A disciple is summoned by Jesus to follow and die. Discipleship entails laying aside self-interest for the sake of other's interests. Jesus urges His disciples to accept the first death rather than the second death from which there is no salvation (Revelation 20:14). Though these words are disturbing, they lead to true life. It is in dying that we find life. "For whoever wants to save his life will lose it, but whoever loses his life for me and for the gospel will save it" (Mark 8:35). Thus, discipleship causes us to die to ourselves and at the same time transforms us for eternity.

Discipleship is costly. To refuse to pay the price, however, is spiritual suicide. The lifestyle of a discipler necessitates the expenditure of all we have for the sake of reproducing additional disciples. While it may cost all, it is also worth all.

Discipleship and Righteousness

One day an exceedingly rich young man approached Jesus and questioned Him, "Good teacher...what must I do to inherit eternal life?" Jesus caught him off guard with His answer, "Why do you call me good? No one is good except God alone" (Mark 10:17,18). In addressing the issue of eternal life, Jesus first dealt with goodness. Apparently this young man thought he was already good. "Was he good enough?" was his concern. Jesus knew we often have a warped sense of what is good and bad like this young man. Our goodness is often self-serving. It fits our situation too neatly at times. Jesus maintained only God was good, and only He could tell us the true meaning of being good.

A righteous person is a good person both in identity and behavior. Even the righteousness we experience is a gift from God. "God made him who had no sin to be sin for us, so that in him we might become the righteousness of God" (2 Corinthians 5:21). We have a new identity, unmerited and free. Is it not incumbent on us to live by God's Spirit so that our outward life might conform to our new nature? With the Lord's help we must strive to match our life-style with our words and intentions. When this occurs we are called people of integrity.

Being a discipler requires we continually reduce any integrity gap. An integrity gap is the difference between our inward and outward lives. We are called upon to model the life of the Spirit before those we disciple. Teaching someone about Jesus is one thing, modeling before them a Christ-like life is something else altogether. If our discipleship is only teaching, then the integrity gap can grow to outrageous proportions. Discipleship is teaching and much more. A disciple must live what is taught, and live in such a way that others are trained in living righteously. Jesus offers and demands upright-ness from Christians. So does discipleship.

Is this call to living righteously the thing that scares so many away from becoming disciplers? Or is it that we fear the infringe-ment upon personal freedom that discipleship brings? Remember, the one who is truly free is free to exercise his freedom and free to not exercise freedom. The one who *must* do what he is free to do is not free. When addressing the topic of a believer's freedom, Paul sets one goal for us all, "whatever you do, do it all for the glory of God" (I Corinthians 10:31). The first motivation for a discipler is to reflect the glory of God. The second motivation Paul says two verses later, "For I am not seeking my own good but the good of many, so that they may be saved." Clearing the road for unbelievers to walk to the Lord motivates Paul. Do we find these as our motivations - living for the glory of God and seeing people saved? They speak to the core of our personal freedom issues. If we choose personal freedom over being a faithful discipler we will run in the face of the Great Commission. Paul caps off this topic in the next verse, "Follow my example, as I follow the example of Christ" (1 Corinthians 11:1). Here is a righteous discipler; he lives for the glory of God first and foremost. He gives his life for the sake of extending the Kingdom of God, and he calls others to follow his example as he yearns toward living in a Christ-like manner.

The rich young man had the option right before him. Jesus offered him true goodness, treasure in heaven and the privilege to follow Him. Sadly, the deceitfulness of riches and individualism entrapped him, and Mark says, "At this the man's face fell. He went away sad, because he had great wealth" (Mark 10:22). He chose temporary riches over eternal treasure, a superficial goodness for true goodness. He chose himself over God and service to His people. Thus, he walked away sad. What will we choose?

Discipleship is Relational

Suggesting that discipleship is a relational process seems self-apparent. For discipling requires at least two believers, (and it is much better with more than two.) The real concern is the quality of the relational connection in the discipling process.

By the very nature of the discipling process, relationships must move to a significant level of depth and maturity for all involved. A wide array of personal concerns must be dealt with in bringing a new believer to maturity in Christ. Morality, lifestyle, consequences of past and present sins, persecution, holiness, life in the Spirit, and new skills for life situations that each Christian must face. Whether the believer is a babe, an adolescent, middle-aged or mature in the Kingdom, we all face these issues. Discipling and being discipled demand these agendas of our lives be addressed together in the light of God's Word and His Spirit.

For a discipling relationship to be effective it must move beyond superficiality, beyond hierarchical structures, beyond talking about ideas and to the deepest levels of appropriate communication. Often the deepest level of communication deals with our emotional response to given situations. Many times the understanding we need involves empathy. You cannot empathize from a distance relationally. It demands relational bonding.

In other words, discipleship is the work of friends. If sensitive issues in a person's life are to come under the Lordship of Christ, then there must be someone they can trust who will walk with them.

I am so deeply indebted to the impact certain people had in my life at the beginning of my ministerial career. Friends literally walked along side me through times of personal confusion and important decisions. Their influence in my life was so profound, I committed myself to understand the power of the love of Christ shared between two individuals. Bruce Larson and Keith Miller were authors I found who exposed me to relational theology. Scripture passages like Romans 12, Philippians 2 and Colossians 3 transformed first my thinking and then my relationships. I learned to "not think of yourself more highly than you ought, but rather think of yourself with sober judgment," to "look not only to your own interests, but also the interests of others," and to "let the word of Christ dwell in you richly as you teach and admonish one another…." Relational theology shaped my understanding of the discipling relationship. Let me state it again, discipleship is the work of close friends.

This aspect of discipleship is highlighted in many forms and contexts throughout this book. When the discipling process becomes relationally stale, the end will soon follow. This has already been addressed with regards to the development of Godly character, and ministering to real needs. Here relational discipleship's correlation to righteous living is highlighted. Relationships that are built on mutual accountability will be promoted. You will find the theme running continually through the student lessons. All of this is quite intentional. The more you understand about communication, relational development, character formation, conflict resolution, ministry equipping and bearing one another's burdens, the more effective you will be as a discipler. Relational dynamics are crucial components in which you will need to investment heavily if you are to see fruitfulness in ministry.

Discipleship is a Process

To be a disciple of Jesus means we give ourselves over to His Lordship. Being a disciple of Jesus reaffirms two things. First, as Paul says in Ephesians 4:5, we all have "one Lord, one faith, one baptism; one God and Father of all, who is over all and through all and in all." Not a variety of gods but one God over all. It is here all believers find their unity. They serve the same Lord. We have all responded to the same act in history. We all listen to the same Spirit.

Secondly, being a disciple of Jesus asserts that each of us is a unique disciple. In this same chapter, Paul contrasts our unity with our diversity, which is highlighted by a variety of differing gifts that come from the same Spirit.

We experience the unity of the Spirit by serving the same Lord, but as we view each other we discover differing gifts and positions in the Father's family. So we experience our unity through our diversity. Our diversity is our strength. It is in this context where Paul talks to us about us growing up into maturity into Christ. Throughout this book, discipleship will be referred to as a process. What Paul was describing in Ephesians is a process. God intends for spiritual growth to occur in a community where the members are diverse and their growth in Him will be unique. A process is different from a program. They even conjure up different mental pictures.

A process could make you think of a parade or procession. As you watch a parade you would see clowns, marching bands, floats, horses and so on. A parade has a great deal of variety and diversity in it. A program brings to mind a person sitting at a desk working through a programmed text looking for specific answers. A process is dynamic while a program seems more static. A process demands flexibility while a program demands uniformity. A process is custom-fit while a program is one-size-fits-all.

A program is always less effective. When we primarily focus on teaching the message of Jesus, we assume knowing the correct doctrine makes a person a mature disciple. We all know by experience that is not true. We could all take a college course on heart surgery, but I'm sure none of us would submit ourselves to the knife of someone who had never performed a successful operation (even if he received straight A's through all this course work). The classroom is essential to the discipling process, but it certainly doesn't encompass it. There must be a supervised residency.

This book does not describe a discipleship program, but rather a process. It does not teach a set plan to take an each disciple through. Rather it tries to show how to become an effective discipler. It does not discard the concept of discipleship programs. On the contrary, these programs are very useful and the lessons teach how to utilize them to their maximum benefit. But the program must be fit to the needs of the person being discipled. And when they no longer "fit" the disciple, a person who understands the discipling process can, with confidence, make the necessary adjustments to continue the process. As you think in terms of the principles that govern the discipling process, you will grow in effectiveness in discipling,

Discipleship must be viewed as an all-encompassing way of life. Being a disciple is first something we <u>are</u> before it is something we <u>do</u>.

Chapter 4

Disciple the Faithful

It was the middle of May and another school term was complete. I sat feeling exhausted from the year. My thoughts darted back and forth. "You would think after eight years of campus ministry; I would begin to see the fruit of my labor. All I feel now is fatigue, and frustration. What happened to me this year? I can't remember working harder, especially these past five months. I did more crisis counseling recently than in probably the previous two to three years. But has anyone really gotten better? In fact, some seem in worse shape. And even my stable students seemed ambivalent at the end of school. Lord, what's going on? Maybe I'm just not cut out to be a campus pastor."

The Lord seemed to lead me to carefully examine my calendar over the last semester. Where had my time gone, and who had I spent it with? Then it began to make sense. I could honestly say that I was a very caring person and the campus ministry was characterized as a loving and safe environment for people with needs. And they came; people with severe needs. I took it upon myself to minister to them all. But they needed much more than what I could provide. Then the next realization dawned. There were several stable and caring students in the campus group, but they were unable to minister to people with deeper needs. At least they felt intimidated by the problems of their brothers and sisters in Christ. I had failed to equip them, making false assumptions that they would be incapable of ministering.

I had repenting to do. I needed to repent for my arrogance that viewed myself as the only one able to care properly, but, most importantly, repentance for failing to enable students to grow as ministers one to another.

Equip the Saints

In the fourth chapter of Ephesians, Paul mentions several leadership gifts in the body of Christ. Throughout chapter four Paul underscores the unity and diversity of the body. Paul believes the unity of the Spirit is maintained and the diversity of the body is liberated, then all members grow into maturity in Christ. However, the way we interpret verse twelve is absolutely crucial to the way we as believers pursue maturity. Some see the role of the leaders mentioned in verse eleven as filling all the responsibilities mentioned in the next two verses. Those being, equipping the saints, doing the works of service, building up the body of Christ, promoting unity, teaching the knowledge of Jesus as the Son of God, and so on. They believe that if they do this, then all the members will become mature.

If, however, you view the role of these leaders as having the primary task of equipping the saints, then ministry becomes available to all members of the body. This view sees every member a minister. The privilege of ministry is open to all, not just to specially trained pastors and vocational staff. Peter says of all members of the community, "but you are a chosen people, a royal priesthood, a holy nation, a people belonging to God, that you may declare the praises of him who called you out of darkness into this wonderful light" (1 Peter 2:9). The priesthood of all believers is taught here. Priests need to be equipped to fulfill their roles. It is the privilege of a pastor to prepare potential leaders for ministry.

2 Timothy 2:2

Beyond the Great Commission, a cardinal passage for discipleship is Paul's words to his disciple and son-in-the-Lord, Timothy. "And the things which you have heard from me in the presence of many witnesses, these entrust to faithful men, who will be able to teach others also" (2 Timothy 2:2, NASB). There are at least four different generations of disciples mentioned in this verse.

Generations	Generation Identified
First	Paul
Second	Timothy
Third	Faithful people
Fourth	Others

This verse illustrates the transgenerational nature of the discipling process. First Paul asks Timothy to recall everything he taught and did which could be verified by witnesses. There is nothing clandestine or esoteric about Paul's ministry. He taught publicly in synagogues, marketplaces, church gatherings and in homes. He prayed for the sick and saw many healed. He cast out evil spirits. He traveled with companions in ministry. (see 2 Timothy 3:10-15) Timothy had been one of those companions. So close had their discipling relationship grown that they even saw each other as father and son. Now Paul tells his disciple to select more faithful disciples from the congregation. He is to select carefully. And in this verse Paul gives a guideline for evaluation of effective ministry. When Timothy witnessed other disciples being equipped from the faithful ones he had equipped, then he could presume success. Discipleship is passing from one generation to another, then to another.

It is often said that, "We cannot have spiritual grandchildren." What is meant is the salvation experience of a parent cannot pass on to the child automatically. Each child must accept Christ volitionally. Of course, this is undisputable. However, when it comes to discipleship, it **is** the goal to produce spiritual grandchildren. You are to disciple in such a way that your disciples will in turn disciple others also. This goal must be kept foremost in our thinking and equipping. You must equip your disciples in such a way that they will be able to disciple someone else later. This is transgenerational discipleship. You have done a good job of discipling when you see your disciple discipling another.

Characteristics of a Faithful Person

Now Paul did not tell Timothy to select any individual to disciple, but to select "faithful" men. Faithful is a key word here. There are at least two characteristics of faithfulness. First, a faithful person is someone who is "full of faith". A full of faith believer is convinced God truly makes a difference in our world. He is someone who believes that prayer in faith can change things. They are full of faith, not in faith itself, but full of faith in Jesus.

A second aspect of faithfulness refers to reliability. A reliable person is someone you can count on. They exhibit consistency in their walk. This is simple evidence of their full-of-faith thinking.

Now, who can be a "faithful man"? Often, we first consider those who have accepted Christ quite some time ago. This is the case in most situations. But some of the most "faith-full" ones are those who have recently come to Christ. A new believer often is newly convinced God truly does make a difference in a person's life. They may or may not have natural leadership abilities, depth of character, or ministry skills, at least probably not yet. Their walk with Christ is not the primary issue. The issue is, are they full of faith? In fact, the whole purpose of the discipling process is to bring them along in their walk with God. Thus, when choosing a disciple, the first question should be, "Are they faithful?"

Let me suggest a principle: Disciple the Faithful, Pastor the Unfaithful

This principle came out of the my experience mentioned at the beginning of this lesson. I discovered that I had spent the vast majority of my time, energy, prayer and counsel upon unfaithful students. At the end of the school year the fruit of unfaithfulness was, sadly, more unfaithfulness. While at the same time there were several very faithful students in the campus group who were neglected. Not only is this principle, "Disciple the Faithful, Pastor the Unfaithful," a valuable insight, it is also prioritizes a pastor's purpose. Prioritize discipling over pastoring. You must never eliminate pastoring, for there will always be those who need you to care for them. Nevertheless, invest the majority of your time, energy, prayer, and equipping on those who are faithful. In doing so you set the Great Commission as a priority in your life.

Some have difficulty with this principle for it seems uncaring to them. However, in fact, it is the most caring thing you can do. To equip the body to minister enables more people to care with effectiveness. Eventually more will find a safe place to heal. At first, you may have to say "no" to some needy people. You may disappoint some. But stay true to this principle, not just for a month or two. Make a long-term commitment to disciple. In my case several of the unfaithful members no longer came to the group (for a varicty of reasons and not directly due to a lack of pastoral attention). A new course was set to work primarily with faithful people. In time, new zeal began to emerge in the campus group. Vision bloomed. Involvement increased. And the next five years of ministry were very encouraging. Steady growth occurred each year. Students who graduated began establishing ministry wherever they moved. They were looked to provide leadership in the local churches they joined. Many students experienced short-term missions outreaches. Some were called into vocational ministry, including campus ministry. Discipling the faithful is the most fruitful thing you can do.

Plato reflected, "A little thing is a little thing, but faithfulness in a little thing becomes a great thing." Selecting a few faithful men and women to disciple may at first seem like a little thing, but God builds it into a great thing.

> *"O lord, you are my God;*
> I will exalt you and praise your name,
> for in perfect faithfulness you have done marvelous things,
> things planned long ago." Isaiah 25:1

Chapter 5

Developing Discipleship in Collegiate Ministry

It is time to move from the philosophical, theological foundations for the discipleship process to the implementation of that process. With us, as with Jesus, the method must result in the building up of believers into disciple-makers. There is no magical recipe. What is needed is a consistent commitment to the process. Remember, discipleship is a process not a program. The principles of discipleship must be applied and tailored to your unique situation. We repeat, there is no magic formula that can be devised to work in all situations.

However, just as a farmer prepares the soil to receive the seed, then fertilizes and waters, so we can prepare the soil of our campus groups to become discipling ministries. Just as with all other ministry, campus ministry is the Lord's work. He causes the growth. He makes people mature. He enlists us to be part of His process. So how can we help prepare the soil? Hopefully some of the following ideas will cultivate your thinking.

Teach on Discipleship

Be careful to instruct students concerning their role in the Great Commission. It is best in a new campus group to use your main meeting as a place to begin teaching on discipleship. One suggestion is to teach through the book of I Thessalonians. You will discover many important principles of discipleship expressed here. This would enable you to teach through a biblical book and the students would receive a picture of the discipling process in the context of this first century congregation.

The students cannot respond without a clear call. As you teach discipleship, pray that the Lord will build a solid vision of discipleship within them. At some point you need to challenge them to become disciples and disciple-makers. A classic book to read at this point is *Dedication and Leadership* by Douglas Hyde. Hyde will challenge you to call for great commitment. Within this book is a set of student lessons for a class on discipleship. Save this material from Hyde's book for a class environment. No doubt you will use some of the concepts in your main meeting teaching, but reserve your large group meeting as a place of worship, teaching and ministry time. You are hoping for a prophetic response from the students to disciple. The class environment is better suited for discussion and interaction.

Develop Discipleship Small Groups

As soon as possible, demonstrate the biblical precedent for large group meetings (for worship, teaching and ministry) and small group meetings (for discipleship, fellowship and accountability). Here is another principle in discipling: People tend to reproduce in ministry and leadership what they have personally experienced.

Students need to experience the discipling process before having it taught to them. They must have a context where they see and experience transparency and affirmation. Do not expect that they can be taught to do something without showing them first how it works.

Therefore, start a discipleship small group and in this group model what they will need to reproduce later as they facilitate small groups. Lead the group with confidence and skill, but also lead in areas that are uncomfortable for you. Lead in skills you feel less able to lead. Show humility in leadership as well as competence. These future leaders will be trying their wings for the first time in many areas of ministry, and they need to see that it is permissible to stumble around a bit before they grow into effectiveness.

Approach this small group with great care. For in this group you will be setting a pattern that will continue for quite some time. That pattern can be a positive pattern (exemplified by commitment, healing, spiritual growth, vision, etc.) or a negative pattern (demonstrated by haphazard preparation, unchallenging, lifeless, impersonal, etc.). This group can be intimidating for the campus pastor who is doing it for the first time. You may need to model several things you have never had a chance to lead before. Study well before you start. Talk to other campus pastors and ask them about their small group experiences. Have a clear plan. Pray hard. And then walk in faith, and see the hand of the Lord bless something very close to His heart - the discipling of students for the Kingdom of God.

Foster an "Every Member a Minister" Organizational Structure

As you are faithful to disciple, you will discover discipleship fosters more ministry opportunities. As students are equipped to assess needs and develop a ministry plan, they will see additional needs and opportunities for ministry. The disciple begins to think creatively and with vision. As they pray, they will sense direction from the Lord.

As you think through your ministry plan, make sure it passes a few tests. Is this campus ministry expandable and flexible? When someone takes on a new ministry responsibility, is that responsibility clearly defined and are the expectations clearly outlined? (A sample job description for a small group leader is included in the appendices.) Are students being pulled into the decision making process for the direction of this campus ministry?

The call to discipleship requires every member see him or herself as a minister within the body of Christ. Once convinced they are called to disciple, they need to know the fellowship group is open to the genuine leading from the Spirit. You need to keep your structures of ministry simple, and not restrictive.

Train Everyone in Message and Method of Discipleship

In the discipling method of Jesus, He clearly selected a few men He would individually disciple. In order to be effective, He restricted

Himself to a certain number for the time He had. However, the call to discipleship was always extended in His teaching and ministry. There is something important for us in this.

As a campus pastor leads the discipling process, he must accomplish two things at the same time. First, he must select faithful individuals to disciple.

This means he must limit himself to certain students in whom to invest time, prayer and training. After sufficient training has occurred and they are leading discipleship small groups, the campus pastor must continue in these relationships to encourage their leadership. He must provide the continuing support they will need.

On the other hand, the campus pastor must be calling the entire body to the discipleship process. Of course, not all will respond to be trained or will go on to service, but nonetheless they must all be offered training.

A very effective means for training the entire campus group is through offering a class on discipleship. This class should be offered during the school week at a time convenient for most students. The campus pastor needs to personally recruit students to attend and be faithful to this class. It will provide an overview of the goals of the campus ministry and describe in detail the discipling process. Experience taught me that this class not only serves to train the faithful, but it begins to build vision in others, as well.

Another important outgrowth of discipling the entire student group is it makes the job of the small group leader easier. How so? If you only train a few select students, you find them to initially be filled with enthusiasm and vision. However, their expectations of what will occur in their discipling relationships and those who have not been trained will be very different. You will end up with many very frustrated small group leaders, and you may lose them due to this frustration. Rather than just train a few, train everyone. Even if only a minority actually become discipleship small group leaders during their college days they will, nevertheless, know what to expect in the discipling process. They will go into their small groups with clearly defined expectations concerning the commitments necessary, how the process will flow, and what the end result should look like. They most importantly will know how they are to function in the group. After being discipled you will find many of these students will later ask to serve as discipling leaders, even though they were reluctant at first.

I discovered it was best to offer the class each school term. I did not allow new freshman to enroll in the class until they had spent at least a semester in the campus ministry and in a small group. The discipleship class will make so much more sense to them if they have had a little history in a small group. They will learn much more if you hold them back a little. I believe it is best to encourage people to <u>experience</u> the discipleship process before they are <u>taught</u> its principles. This may seem counter-intuitive, but their fresh experience will give them a context with which to more quickly and accurately comprehend the principles.

Then you must promote the class vigorously. Do it face to face. Send them a personal letter. Use student testimonies of those who have taken the class previously. Be creative and be persistent. Your personal involvement is crucial to successful disciple-making.

Select Discipling Leaders and Support their Development

Essential to the discipling process is the recruitment, training and appointment of discipling student leaders. More specifics on this process will be covered in the next two chapters.

At this point let's look at a few issues. In the beginning stages of a new campus ministry, it is the campus pastor's goal to affirm students to leadership in the group. This increases their ownership in the fellowship and is very valuable for growth. But what kind of leader is needed? Some tend to select leaders who have a focus of ministry over the whole fellowship group. They are an extension of the campus pastor's role. A generalist leader gives direction to the entire campus ministry.

I recommend the first student leaders selected in a new or small campus ministry be discipling leaders. A campus pastor can continue to provide the overall direction of a small campus group. Selecting discipling student leaders more quickly reproduces ministry, and more growth will probably come from discipling leaders than from generalist student leaders.

The discipling student leader is the key leader, no matter how young or old, big or small a campus ministry. Other kinds of leadership roles will come and go in campus ministry, but the discipling leader is essential at all times. When their role is devalued or de-emphasized, the campus ministry will begin to suffer; if not immediately, within one or two school years.

The campus pastor must insure these leaders are carefully selected, thoroughly trained, and then cared for on a continuing basis. As a campus ministry grows to over 40 in small groups, you may need to consider using students who have proven themselves effective in discipleship to serve as leaders for other small group leaders. Beyond the campus pastor, the discipling student leader may need other students to support them in their role of ministry. Some campus groups have called this student discipleship specialist a discipling resource leader. (See appendix for Resource Leader Job Description).

The development of a discipling campus ministry is an on-going process, especially in the university setting. With the high turnover in membership the need to select, train and supervise is constant. Failing to give prime attention to this process for even one school year can have serious repercussions down the road. There are a few major things working against you in this process. Several aspects in discipleship run completely contrary to the university culture. Lack of commitment, accountability and maturity are areas that represent hindrances to developing discipling leaders. Because of these factors, and others, the discipling process may be frustrated.

On the other hand, it is the heart of the Great Commission. Jesus inaugurated it and then commended it. He is still committed to seeing it accomplished. You can be confident you are leading with the Lord's favor when you give yourself to discipleship. Just be sure to faithfully disciple vigorously each school year. Also rest assured Jesus will equip you and the Holy Spirit will change the hearts of reluctant students to see the Great Commission carried out on your university.

Chapter 6

Selecting Leaders for Discipleship

The campus ministry was only a few months old, but graciously it had a good beginning. The campus pastor and his wife were able to start (between them) three discipleship small groups with four to five in each small group. About a month before finals of the fall semester, a weekend retreat was held with most of the students attending. The retreat topic: The Discipleship Process.

After much prayer the campus pastor went into the next main weekly meeting ready to challenge the young group to become a committed discipling campus ministry. The meeting focused on the students giving their reflections and reactions to the retreat. Then the pastor asked, "Do we desire to become that kind of a ministry?" After some contemplation and pointed dialogue the consensus was "Yes".

The pastor told them the next logical step was to select and train students to lead the existing small groups. He then laid out specifically the level of commitment necessary to become a discipling small group leader. Between leading the small group, preparing for the small group, a leadership meeting for training and oversight, main weekly meetings, Sunday local church attendance, and one-on-one times with small group members, it appeared that 15 hours per week would be necessary.

Then the pastor said, "I will accept applications to interview for these leadership positions. Do not ask to interview if you know you are unable to comply with all the necessary requirements to lead. If you are for some reason (like part-time work, excessive school load, etc.) unable to fulfill all the requirements then don't apply. Your application assumes your willingness to do whatever is necessary to become an effective discipler."

There were about twenty students in the campus group at this time. It was an act of faith to ask for that kind of commitment from the outset. Some might say "Start smaller and grow into it." Douglas Hyde in his book *Dedication and Leadership* advocates challenging people to large and meaningful action. "if you make mean little demands upon people, you will get a mean little response which is all you deserve, but if you make big demands on them, you will get a heroic response...work off the assumption that if you call for big sacrifices people will respond to this and, moreover, the relatively smaller sacrifices will come quite naturally." The twenty had a week to prayerfully consider and respond if they would like to apply. It was a very important moment for the future of this fledgling university group.

Amazingly, fourteen out of the twenty interviewed, and from these, five were affirmed to leadership. They each voluntarily decided to cut their school class loads back by one class to be more free to disciple. They each fulfilled the stated minimum requirements and they all did a great job of leading. From that point and for over ten years this campus group has had a continuing supply of committed small group disciplers. The requirements, though stated, did not need to be heavily stressed, for everyone witnessed the commitment of their small group leader while they were still small group members. A standard had been established and it reproduced itself year after year.

The Essential Makeup of a Disciple-maker

What criteria do you use in selecting a small group discipler? Obviously, it is a matter of sincere prayer and of discerning the Lord's will, but what do you pray about? What are the essentials you expect to see in these student leaders? This is answered in detail in the Student Lesson 12. Also see chapter 1 of this book.

Look for these five essentials:

- a student who is developing in Godly character
- a student who has a pastoral heart
- a student who exhibits vision for ministry
- a student who is full of zeal for the Lord and wholeheartedly committed to Jesus
- a student who has a measure of ministry skills

More often than not we elevate ministry skills in prospective discipling leaders to be of first and foremost importance. We look for the ability to lead worship, lead a Bible study, and pray with others. However, it is better to look for evidences of the first four essentials. They indicate growth in godliness. These are the kind of students you want influencing other students. Ministry skills can be taught. My recommendation is to look first for inward qualities before looking for outward skills.

The Interviewing Process

Someone once commented, "Why go through all the trouble of interviewing? Why don't you just pick 'em?" Having the campus pastor personally appoint discipling leaders would be easier and quicker, but again we must be reminded that discipleship is a process. There are important factors involved in an interview and selection process that are healthy for the ones being interviewed and for the entire campus group. Here are some suggested stages for the interviewing process.

1) Clearly define the responsibility

Make sure the student has a clear understanding of the responsibility they are applying for. A job description should be made available. A sample is offered in the appendices. It should clearly outline the expectations and qualifications necessary to serve. Try not to assume anything. This will help prevent misunderstanding and disappointment down the road.

2) Invite students to interview

The students need an opportunity to pray about this issue, and then to affirm their desire to serve. This causes them to count the cost of discipleship. When they ask to interview, it normally is an indication they have taken this matter seriously. Sometimes the campus pastor will have a few students in mind that she/he feels would make good disciplers. The campus pastor should feel free to talk to them about interviewing. Do not coerce them, but talk with them about becoming a discipler and what that may mean for them. Even those who have previously served as small group leaders before should ask to interview again. This review of their previous service is very helpful. It gives you a chance to address any on-going development concerns you have with this student's leadership.

3) Establish an interview format

Insure this process is impartial. In a beginning campus ministry the campus pastor may need to select the first group of discipleship small group leaders (as was done in the illustration above). This is not ideal, but may be necessary the first time. If possible, find one or two others who could assist you in interviewing. Possibilities might include an associate pastor from a local church, a mature layman who has a campus ministry background, or a graduate student who would not have the time to lead a small group, but is a mature believer and could join you on an interview committee.

Once a campus ministry has student leaders, then use some of them on your interviewing committee. Ask those who seem to have the concepts of discipleship well in mind and were effective in leading their small groups. Many campus groups use the last three to four weeks of the school year to do their interviews for the next school year. If this is done, then student leaders who are finishing a year of serving will have fresh ideas and questions to ask potential leaders. This also gives the new leaders the summer break to prepare themselves for the next year.

It would be helpful if you developed an interview form your committee could use. This will provide some uniformity. However, feel free to ask questions that would be unique to the person before you. A sample interview form is provided in the appendices. Most interviews take about 20 - 30 minutes. It is good to pray with each one who interviews before they leave. This gives the committee an immediate chance to thank God for what He has done in the student's life. This whole process is intended to be an edifying experience for the student, not an inquisition.

4) Build integrity in the selection process

Here is a suggestion. Ask the committee members not to discuss any of the interviews with each other or anyone else until the committee meets again. Give about four days to a week after the last interview, for the committee members to pray and think about all of the interviews. When the entire committee comes together after this break, have them cast a ballot on each person before they discuss any of the interviews. Only at this point discuss the interviews as a committee.

Then discuss every interview. Those you affirmed unanimously should be discussed to see why the committee members affirmed them. The same should be done for those who were unanimously not affirmed. Those with a split vote should be discussed, and then a consensus needs to be arrived at as to which direction to go. Should they be affirmed, or held back for a time? The details of these discussions need to remain in the confidence of the committee members and not made public knowledge.

5) Give feedback to everyone who interviews

Now the selections have been made, it is important to go to every student who interviewed and discuss with them the reflections of the selection committee. Those who are affirmed to serve need to know what the committee saw as their strengths. This is a great opportunity to bless what God has done in a person. No doubt there will be some areas of concern, even for a student who has been affirmed. Here you can highlight where spiritual, emotional or behavioral growth needs to occur. As you can see, this process itself can serve as a discipling process for all who interview.

All those who were not affirmed need to receive feedback as well, maybe even more than those affirmed. For campus pastors who fear conflict, this may be an intimidating process. In most cases, however, it is a special time to specifically love a person and call them on to growth in Christ. The feedback is almost always appreciated. Only those who are very insecure may have difficulty with the evaluation, but this in itself may be healing for them if the approach to them is with loving concern. Usually only one person should give the feedback. Any committee member can be used. It may, however, be most appropriate for the campus pastor to do the feedback for those not affirmed. This demands maturity. Not only can you give feedback, but you may also give suggestions and loving support to those who interviewed on how they can grow in Christ.

6) Commission the affirmed leaders publicly

At either the last main meeting of the year, or at one of the first meetings of the new school year, take time to call each one who is to serve as a discipling small group leader before the whole campus fellowship. At this point pray and commission them to the task before them. Let the entire group participate in this process.

By this time, the student has affirmed him/herself by asking to interview. Mature leaders in the group have affirmed them. The body through prayer has affirmed them. And, obviously, everyone along the way is praying for the Lord's direction. Thus, the student begins to serve knowing they have everyone's backing. For a new leader (as well as old leaders) this support and affirmation means a great deal. It is intended to give them a strong boost of confidence at the start.

In the campus ministry used in this illustration, many students return after graduation and state that the interviewing process was very valuable to them. Not only did it have direct bearing on their spiritual development, but it also prepared them for the world they moved into after college. Many found themselves interviewing for careers and they discovered they were well prepared for this new stage in their lives. Discipleship is a process that builds people spiritually and in many other ways, as well.

Chapter 7

Supervising and Supporting the Discipleship Leaders

Consider this scenario. Student leaders are well trained and commissioned. They passed all the requirements to serve as discipleship leaders. They found at a handful of students and they set out to make disciples. But shortly, they begin to feel disheartened and later overwhelmed. They feel neglected. You then find them sitting in your office, giving you a rationale for why they need to resign from their leadership role.

In the Great Commission Jesus closed with the words, "And surely I am with you always, to the very end of the age." Now we are not like Jesus. We cannot be with the student leaders 24/7. Nevertheless they need the support and continued enabling to carry out their responsibilities. The new leaders are experiencing things in their Christian walk they never encountered before. They are performing some ministry skills for the first time and encountering needs in people they have never dealt with before. They feel a distance between them and small group members they never felt before.

They encounter increased spiritual warfare. They're successful, but then deal with the ugly head of pride. Their idealism is dealt a blow by the realism of their new situation. If they do not have a mature leader to go to as a sounding board, someone to trouble shoot issues with, someone to care for their personal needs, and someone to sharpen their skills to enable them to become even more effective, then their vision will eventually dim. They could become disillusioned and despair over whether they were ever meant to disciple.

The Minister's Role in Supervision

The campus pastor is now fulfilling important roles in the discipling process at three different levels.

- **Challenging** the whole group to discipleship, building a vision in them and providing training for them all.
- **Equipping** some to prepare them for the discipling role.
- **Supervising** those already leading to keep them healthy and encouraged.

Concerning this third level of supervision there are three areas of supervision that should be considered:

Pastoral Care

This is individual care for the personal needs of the discipling leader. Their own lives continue on. They face new challenges in their academic pursuits. Often they are building significant relationships that demand increased time commitments. Family matters, financial pressures, and increased stress are among the issues they encounter. They will no doubt be sharing many of these things in their small group. However, several of the group members may be young in the lord. Though it is no one's fault, the student leader may feel unsupported, even within their small group. It is important for the campus pastor to spend time with the leaders individually, talking to them about what they are doing apart from their discipleship concerns. Make sure they know they are important as individuals beyond their leadership roles in the group.

Continuous Development

It is impossible to anticipate all the issues a discipler will face as they lead. Theory is replaced by the actual. At this stage valuable discipling by the campus pastor should occur. Talk through the situations they are facing, and brainstorm together about how to respond. In doing so you are teaching them how to approach ministry. They begin to understand the process of discipleship more as you spend time with them. You can also pull all the discipleship leaders together and teach various skills or refine previously taught skills. Provide materials for them to read for leadership development. They are in a wonderful position to learn and grow. Before, you were giving them all the answers. Now they are learning all the questions. They are at a very receptive time to integrate a philosophy of ministry with a practice in ministry.

Assessment

Ministry is a very difficult thing to evaluate. Was it a good teaching or not? Did I do a good job leading worship or counseling? These questions haunt every minister, and they are heightened in the new student leader. They feel like novices and need honest, positive feedback. Help them learn how to do good self-evaluation. Be careful to observe my "three-for-one rule": give three comments of affirmation for every one comment of correction. This rule not only applies for new leaders but is valuable to offer your senior pastor at your local church, as well. Assessment is only valuable when it is heard. If leaders know they will only receive corrective critiques, they will probably shy away from assessment opportunities.

Support

As mentioned in the interviewing chapter, it is helpful to establish the leadership selection process in the late spring. Then, throughout the summer, the campus pastor should stay in touch with them. It would be a good time to give them a summer reading list that will prepare for the fall. During the summer, or just before the beginning of the fall term, hold a retreat for discipleship leaders only. Orient them to the fall schedule and review essential skills and goals that pertain to the first six weeks of school. It is valuable for them to get back in touch with each other relationally. Maybe they had a difficult and demanding summer, and a time together for refreshing worship and prayer is very encouraging.

During the school year, your oversight needs to be both one-to-one and in groups of leaders. The one-to-one times serve best for personal care and assessment. The group meetings best assist continued enabling. Determine the regularity most feasible in your campus situation. You need to stay current with your leaders to truly provide hands-on supervision.

Here's an observation: in a campus ministry with eight or fewer discipling leaders invite everyone to attend the leadership meetings. When you have more than eight, you will be best served by breaking them down into subgroups of leaders (maybe men's and women's groups). At this point you need additional help in providing leader supervision. Some campus ministries might add a campus ministry staff person with a major share of their responsibility going to coordinate these leaders. In many other cases you will need to use mature student leaders who have had experience in leading. They could coordinate a smaller group of leaders (maybe three to six), and then report back to the campus pastor. Some campus groups call these smaller leadership groups Resource Groups, and the coordinator of them Resource Leaders.

One last thing: It is important to recognize the efforts of student leaders. At an appropriate time during the year, maybe at the end of the school year, have some means to show appreciation to these leaders for their service. Give honor where honor is due, and these students should be honored. This will encourage them and will demonstrate to the entire student group that this capacity is highly esteemed. It will foster a greater desire for others to follow in their path.

Part Two

Leadership Training for Discipleship

A Practical Guide for Developing Discipleship Small Groups

The following twelve lessons are intended to serve as the foundation for small group discussions. Many students find it is best used when a chapter or two is read prior to or during a gathering of a handful of students and then discussed a section at a time. A teacher is always beneficial, but not in a talking-head format. A teacher who is an effective disciple-maker can facilitate these discussions and encourage students to learn by group-discovery.

The following generic discussion questions will serve these lessons well. Also, please note the suggestions mention in this book in the section titled, **How to Use this Book.**

- What scriptural underpinning supports this section?
- How do these statements change my pre-conditioning and presuppositions?
- What do I need to do to apply these principles in my life?
- How does this affect my understanding of the personal nature of God?
- What am I learning about God's mission in the world?
- What is the main takeaway for me from this lesson?

- What is God's Spirit saying to me through this study on discipleship?
- How will I participate in The Great Commission?

Lesson 1

A Biblical Foundation For Discipleship

A Philosophy of Ministry for the University

A. Community

Our Goal is to become a "community" of students on campus. We put a high priority on coming together as a group for biblically commanded activity. God has intended for us to come to a greater understanding of Him by vital interaction in the Body of Christ.

"Well, Mr. Curtis, it seems your inability to function stems from the fact that you are a disembodied head."

This means that we can experience fully what God has for us only when we are in the context of "community." Only in the Body can the gifts of the Holy Spirit find meaning. Only in the Body can multifaceted ministry best occur. Scattered Bible studies alone are not sufficient for a full and balanced growth in Christ. What is necessary is a fully operating Body with leadership, prayer, training, worship, fellowship, and outreach.

B. Community has three primary characteristics:

1. Proximity

Students should consider living in proximity with each other as a great aid in the development of community. During times of revival the Church has gravitated to communes many times in its history. The attempt is to promote a community with purity as its purpose, and unified witness as its goal. Close proximity is valuable to building community (having students concentrated in a few dorm complexes can be a great asset), however it does not guarantee true community will exist.

2. Relationships

Whereas proximity focuses on the frequency of being together, effective community focuses on how concurrent people are in their relationships. The quality and depth of sharing one to another has a much bigger bearing upon community then mere association.

3. Focus

Every community must have a focus or reason to be. For Christians their focus must be Christ. If it is not, they are Christians merely gathering together to create a social bond.

C. Key Ingredients for Community: A Sample Covenant Among Believers

1. Affirmation

There is nothing you have done or will do that will make me stop loving you. I may not agree with your actions, but I will love you as a person and do all I can to hold you up in God's affirming love.

2. Availability

Anything I have – time, energy, insight, possessions – is at your disposal if you need it, to the limit of my resources.

3. Prayer

I commit to pray for you regularly, believing that our caring Father wishes His children to pray for one another and ask Him for the blessings they need.

4. Openness

I promise to strive to become a more open person, disclosing my feelings, my struggles, my joys, and hurts to you as well as I am able. This is to affirm your worth to me as a person. In other words, I need you!

5. Honesty

I will try to mirror back to you what I am hearing you say and feel. If this means risking pain for either of us, I will trust our relationship enough to take that risk, realizing it is in "speaking the truth in love that we grow up in every way in Christ who is the head." (Ephesians 4:15)

6. Sensitivity

Even as I desire to be known and understand by you, I commit to be sensitive to you and to your needs to the best of my ability. I will try to hear you, see you, and feel where you are and to draw you out from discouragement or withdrawal.

7. Confidentiality

I will promise to keep confidential whatever is shared in order to provide the atmosphere of trust necessary for openness.

8. Accountability

I am accountable to you to become what God has designed me to be in His loving creation.

"It's been brought to my attention that there's been too much idle talk going on. Let me just say right now – I won't have any gossiping old hens in *this* church."

D. The Biblical Foundation for the Philosophy

"They devoted themselves to the apostles *teaching*, and to *fellowship*, to the *breaking of bread*, and to *prayer*...Every day they continued to *meet together* in the temple courts. They *broke bread* in their homes and *ate together* with glad and sincere hearts, *praising God* and enjoying favor of all the people. And the *Lord added* to their number daily those who were being saved." (Acts 2:42, 46-47)

The italicized words highlight the aspects of Chi Alpha's five-fold philosophy:

- *teaching* — discipleship
- *fellowship* — fellowship
- *breaking of bread* — fellowship

- *prayer* — prayer
- *meet together* — fellowship
- *broke bread* — fellowship
- *ate together* — fellowship
- *praising God* — worship
- *Lord added* — mission

E. The Focus of the Philosophy is Christian Growth

Each aspect (worship, prayer, fellowship, discipleship, and mission) produces health and growth both for individual believers and for the body of Christ. Each of us giving continual attention to these aspects throughout our lives while we are in an accountable Christian community will keep us on the narrow path that leads to our Father's house.

F. A Strategy for Implementing the Philosophy

"Our primary strategy is to work toward the building of a group or community of people who share the ideals of becoming a community of worship, a community of prayer, a community of fellowship, a community of discipleship, and a community of mission. We believe the most fertile atmosphere for people to come to faith and maturity in Christ is warm exposure to a group of people fervently committed to the God of the Bible, to one another, and to the task of evangelizing the campus. As a worshipping, loving, praying, discipling, witnessing community, they demonstrate the Kingdom of God and most effectively enculturate others in it." (Chi Alpha Philosophy)

Our Particular Emphasis Here is Discipleship

A. Christ calls us to disciple the nations.

"All authority in heaven and on earth has been given to me. Therefore go and make disciples of all nations, baptizing them in the name of the Father and of the Son and of the Holy Spirit, and teaching them to obey everything I have commanded you. And surely I will be with you always, to the very ends of the age." (Matthew 28:18-20)

"But you will receive power when the Holy Spirit comes on you; and you will be my witnesses in Jerusalem, and in all Judea and Samaria, and to the ends of the earth." (Acts 1:8)

The scope of the Christ' call:

- Purpose: "make disciples of all nations"
- Program: "teaching them to obey everything I have commanded you"
- Provision: "you will receive power when the Holy Spirit comes on you"
- Promise: "And surely I will be with you always, to the very end of the age."

Let There Be No Misunderstanding at This Point

Discipling is a task that requires much more than simple programs or techniques. Discipling at all times requires the power and presence of Jesus Christ through the indwelling Spirit!

B. Christ entrusted the Kingdom of God into the men He discipled.

He didn't write a holy book, He left no manual, no tablets full of commandments, only trained, changed and empowered men to continue His mission – to save the world.

"What do we have in the church today that the early church did not have?" What can you think of beyond hymnals, buildings, Bibles, and paid staff?

"What do we have (or could we have) today that they did have in the early church?" As we saw in Acts 2, they had each other and the ability to worship and share the Lord with each other. They had the kind of relationships that are described in the "Key Ingredients for Community." The kingdom of God is a kingdom of changed, transformed people who share the Lord with each other and with the world. Thus, discipleship is relationships built on Jesus.

C. Christ demonstrated that discipleship must be encased in a personal, relational model and not in a static educational mode.

This calls for the direct personal involvement of the discipler in the lives of those being discipled. "You did not choose me, but

I chose you and appointed you to go and bear fruit – fruit that will last…This is my command: Love each other." (John 15:16,17)

"It is our conviction that discipling is best accomplished in the relational context of the more matured believer helping to nurture younger members of the community." (Chi Alpha Philosophy)

To Summarize

The making of disciples is not something that just happens. It is a very deliberate and specific process requiring strategy, time, and prayer. It is a process by which growing Christians impart their knowledge and experience in the Lord Jesus to newer Christians in the context of personal relationships. By this process each member is thus given the basic knowledge and skills necessary to grow toward maturity in Christ and is equipped for the work of the ministry. (Ephesians 4:11-16)

We desire to follow the instructions of Paul to Timothy, "the things which you have heard from me in the presence of many witnesses, these entrust to faithful men, who will be able to teach others also." (2 Timothy 2:2) In this way we perpetuate a continuous development of maturing leaders for the work of Christ here in our campus ministry, then across our state, our nation, and through our mission endeavors, around the world. For review please see chapter 4 **Disciple the Faithful.**

The Purpose of Discipleship in a Campus Ministry Setting

A. Provide all students involved with this ministry a spiritual/pastoral discipler for continued Christian growth and nurture.
B. Provide every student a core of fellow students in which to share the love of God with each other.
C. Provide a relational learning experience in the practices of the Christian faith.
D. Provide an atmosphere for leadership development among students for God's kingdom work.
E. Provide for the continual development of transgenerational ministry in the university community.

Lesson 2

The Master's Method I: Selection & Association

The Importance of His Method

"The days of His flesh were by the unfolding in time of the plan of God from the beginning. It was always before His mind. He intended to save out of the world a people for Himself and to build a church of the Spirit which would come in glory and in power. This world was His by creation, but He did not seek to make it His permanent abiding place. His mansions were in the sky. He was going to prepare a place for His people that had foundations eternal in the heavens.

No one was excluded from His gracious purpose. His love was universal. Make no mistake about it. He was the Savior of the world. (John 4:42) God wanted all men to be saved and to come to a knowledge of the truth. To that end Jesus gave Himself to provide a salvation from all sin for all men. In that He died for one, He died for all. Contrary to our superficial thinking, there never was a distinction in His mind between home and foreign missions. To Jesus it was all world evangelism.

His life was ordered by His objective. Everything He did and said was a part of the whole pattern. It had significance because it contributed to the ultimate purpose of His life in redeeming the world for God. This was the motivating vision governing His behavior. His steps were ordered by it. Mark it well. Not for one moment did Jesus lose sight of His goal.

That is why it is so important to observe the way Jesus maneuvered to achieve His objective. The Master disclosed God's strategy of world conquest. He had confidence in the future precisely because He lived according to that plan in the present. There was nothing haphazard about His life – no wasted energy, not an idle word. He was on business for God (Luke 2:49). He lived, He died, and He rose again according to schedule. Like a general plotting His course of battle, the Son of God calculated to win. He could not afford to take a chance. Weighing every alternative and variable factor in human experience, he conceived a plan that would not fail." *Robert E. Coleman Master Plan of Evangelism (Revell, Old Tappan, NJ, 1963) 17-18*

Discussion questions

Q: Jesus had a mission to save the world. During His ministry He never left a geographical area larger than the state of New Jersey. Did He accomplish His goal to save the world? If so, in what ways?

Q: What does Coleman mean that Jesus never had a distinction between home and foreign missions? What significance is there in this statement?

Q: How does having a clear plan and confidence in that plan help us know how we are to live today?

Q: What does this mean, "If you do a good job at home, it will go around the world!"?

Is Bigger Always Better?

Often our culture associates successful enterprises as those endeavors that end up being large and wealthy. This tendency has also gripped portions of the Church of Jesus Christ. We too often associate numbers as somehow equaling success, or we associate a large prosperous building as somehow showing God's blessing is on a particular ministry.

It should be understood living things do grow and there is nothing intrinsically wrong with large churches. But these things do not in and of themselves show God's blessing or spiritual success. One need only look at the growth and wealth of some cult groups to see we would be hard pressed if this were our only criterion.

Instead we must search out the principles guiding Jesus' ministry and determine his goals. Rather than meeting the world's criteria for success, it is in the faithful fulfillment of God's commands and purposes that make us truly successful.

It should be our conviction that we should not only be students of Jesus' words but also of Jesus' methods. The Scripture is not only our message book but also our method book when it comes to the life of Christ.

Is Discipling the Best Way to Reach the World?

Let's look at two possible ways to evangelize. First, let's look for a Super Evangelist (SE). We'll pray for Super Evangelist, provide for all of Super Evangelist's material needs, and book meetings ahead city after city. We'll do everything in order for Super Evangelist to concentrate exclusively on evangelism. If the fruit of the Super Evangelist's labor are 1,000 people converted each and every day for 10 years, how many would be saved through this incredible campaign?

Now, let's take one equally committed person who would share the Lord throughout the normal course of day-to-day activities and would see 5 conversions a year. We'll call this person Faithful Discipler (FD). Not only will Faithful Discipler lead people to Christ, but he will train them to share their faith just as freely as he had with them. Faithful Discipler will spend a year discipling the 5 new converts and then in the next year those disciples would each reach and disciple 5 others. If this process were to occur over 10 years, how many would be saved after this manner?

	Year 1	**Year 5**	**Year 10**
SE	365,000	1,825,000	3,650,000
FD	6	3750	11,718,750

Beyond, the numerical advantage, what other advantages would there be for the mission of the Church to the Faithful Discipler model? What can you think of beyond these ideas?

- This method does not rely on the success or failure of just one individual.
- The results here are not just converts but disciples and disciplers!
- It follows the model of Jesus.
- Retention is much higher by discipleship.
- The potential transformation of the disciple's life is profound.
- Faithful discipleship is feasible.
- Discipleship is less expensive.

SELECTION: People Where His Method

Coleman reminds us before Jesus ever preached His first sermon He had already selected people to follow Him. Jesus was not interested in developing programs that would reach the multitudes, but in developing individuals the multitudes would follow.

The men He selected would not impress us as being "key people." (Nor did they impress the religious leaders of Jesus' day). They were rowdy, insensitive, quarrelling, envious and bigoted. They came from common backgrounds. A few were even social outcasts. Within these individuals He established the Kingdom of God on earth.

What we think the disciples were like.

What the disciples were really like.

Just think what a modern management consultant might say about Jesus' choice of associates. Check out this consulting report.

HUMAN RESOURCES SPECIALISTS

Date: AD 30
To: Jesus, Son of Joseph
Woodcrafter Carpenter Shop
Nazareth, 25922
From: Jordan Personnel Management Consultants
Jerusalem 22312

Dear Sir:

Thank you for submitting the resumes of the twelve men you picked for the management positions in your new organization. All of them have taken a battery of tests. We have not only run the results through our computer, but have also arranged personal interviews for each of them with our expert psychologist and vocational aptitude consultant.

The profiles of all tests are included, and you will want to study each of them carefully. As part of our service, and for your guidance, we make some general statements. This is given as a result of staff consultations and comes without any additional fee.

It is our staff's opinion that most of your nominees are lacking in background education and vocational aptitude for the type of enterprise you are undertaking. They do not have the modern team concept. We would recommend you continue your search for persons of experience, with managerial ability and a proven track record.

Simon Peter is emotionally unstable and given to fits of violent temper. Andrew has absolutely no qualities of leadership. The two brothers, James and John, the sons of Zebedee, place personal interest above company loyalty. Thomas demonstrates a questioning attitude that would tend to undermine others' morale. We feel it is our duty to tell you that Matthew has been blacklisted by the Greater Jerusalem Better Business Bureau. James, the son of Alphaeus, and Thaddeus definitely have radical tendencies and they both registered a high score on the manic-depressive profile.

One of the candidates, however, shows great potential. He is a man of broad ability and resourcefulness, meets people well, has a keen business mind and has contacts in high places. He is highly motivated, ambitious and responsible. We recommend Judas Iscariot as your controller and right-hand man. All of the other profiles are self-explanatory.

We wish you every success in your new venture.

Sincerely,
Human Resource Specialists

Carl was determined not to be stereotyped as just another dumb ox.

Nevertheless, the people Jesus chose did have some positive qualities. They were:

- **Teachable**: they were honest, and willing to confess their need for understanding
- **Sincere**: they truly wanted to know and serve God
- **Hungry**: they were tired of the emptiness of their present religious life

Jesus taught us by His methods that the world may be transformed, but only as individuals of the world are transformed. He also showed us anyone is a candidate to be a discipler. It is not so much an issue of whether you are able to disciple, but whether you are willing to disciple.

Are there any distinctive characteristics in how Jesus related to people? Certainly not in compassion, but truly there were distinctions in the amount of time Jesus spent with different groups of people, the depth of teaching different groups received, and the difference in levels of commitment. Noting that Jesus purposed to work through individuals, let's look at the specifics of exactly how he went about it. These distinctions move from the least amount of time (outermost sphere of influence) to the most time invested (innermost sphere of influence).

The Multitudes: In the early part of Jesus ministry, we see him having fruitful ministry among crowds of people. He did not turn away from the needs of the many. He felt responsible for their overwhelming pressing needs.

The 500: Paul tells us Jesus, after His resurrection, appeared to 500 people at one time. Surely these must have been followers of the Lord. It is significant that the Lord of the universe had ministered for over three years among the same nation of people and was killed and then rose from the dead! After this he could only raise a crowd of 500! It does not appear to be a powerful, world-shaking movement, does it? Yet Jesus felt confident He had finished all that the Father had sent Him to do. He left behind a small core of trained individuals to continue His mission to reach the world through continued discipleship.

The 120: Just after the Ascension, Luke records there were at least 120 people who were willing to follow Jesus' wishes to go to Jerusalem and pray.

The 70: In Luke 10, it is recorded Jesus sent out 70 disciples. In what capacity they were disciples is not explained, neither what level of relationship, nor how they were trained.

The Twelve: These men were with Jesus from almost the beginning of His ministry. They were with Him, heard Him, prayed with Him, and He loved them and trained them. They knew each other very well.

The Three: Peter, James and John were within the Twelve. They experienced things the rest of the Twelve did not. John was called the "beloved disciple." These three seem to be the most important and significant relationships in Jesus' life (beyond this immediate family).

As disciple-makers we need to relate at levels like Jesus:

The Multitudes: We need to respond to the needs of the world at large. Social concern and community service should exemplify our faith.

500/120: This might be descriptive of our relationships in a local church.

70: This is probably the maximum number of concurrent relationships we can maintain at any one time in our lives.

12: This represents the maximum number of depth relationships we can keep concurrent. It could represent our small group.

3: It is important that we invest ourselves in a few (or best friends).

In our relationships, we must develop realistic expectations. We tend to either expect too much or too little of both others and ourselves. When we expect all relationships to be really deep and meaningful, we may be creating frustration for ourselves. Selection demands that we choose. We must choose to be transparent to some. On the other hand, we must extend love to all as Jesus did. The limits of Jesus' selection did not reflect a limit of His love. He selected some for the purpose of depth discipleship. Aligning our expectations with Jesus' model of life will bring spiritual health to us.

"One must decide where he wants his ministry to count – in the momentary applause of popular recognition or in the reproduction of his life in a few chosen individuals who will carry on his work after he has gone. Really it is a question of which generation we are serving." *The Master Plan of Evangelism* 37

ASSOCIATION: He Stayed With Them

Beyond selecting people, Coleman points out that Jesus needed followers who could bear witness to His life and ministry and carry on after He returned to the Father.

It is important to see Jesus' disciples were not taught in a classroom and then asked to recite their lessons in Doctrine 101 and Practical Theology 212, but discipleship with Jesus meant that class was always in session. They didn't learn doctrine. They participated in doctrine.

And as time went on, rather than giving less time to the Twelve, he actually gave more. As the final days of Jesus' ministry approached, the intensity of Jesus' time with the disciples even magnified. The probable application for us from this example of Jesus is that some strategy must be found whereby every convert is given a Christian friend to follow until such time as he can lead another.

How may the principles of Selection and Association be implemented in your campus ministry? Can you brainstorm other ideas beyond these?

- Arrange for a campus ministry roommate.
- Select a few dorms where most campus ministry members can live in proximity with each other and share the same food service.
- Move back into the dorm.
- Develop off-campus separate community houses for men and women.
- Take classes together.
- Invite one another to go shopping.
- Play sports together, create an intramural coed team.
- Become prayer partners.
- Join or create ministry teams, i.e. provide social functions, develop an evangelism committee, create a drama group, build worship teams.
- Provide hospitality in your off campus apartment for your campus ministry friends who need a break from dorm life.

Lesson 3

The Master's Method II: Consecration, Impartation & Delegation

CONSECRATION: Carry Your Own Cross

The following letter highlights the topic of consecration. Read it and then discuss together. This is a letter from a revolutionary to his fiancée to explain why he was breaking their engagement.

> "We revolutionaries have a high casualty rate. We are the ones who get shot and hung and ridiculed and fired from our jobs and in every way made as uncomfortable as possible. A certain percentage of us get killed or imprisoned. We live in virtual poverty. We turn back to the party every penny we make above what is absolutely necessary to keep us alive.

> We revolutionaries do not have the time or the money for many movies, concerts, T-bone steaks, or decent homes or new cars. We have been described as fanatics. We are fanatics. Our lives are dominated

by one great overshadowing fact: the struggle for world dominion.

We revolutionaries have a philosophy of life no amount of money can buy. We have a cause to fight for, a definite purpose in life. We subordinate our petty personal selves into the great movement of humanity. And if our personal lives seem hard, or our egos appear to suffer through subordination to the party, then we are adequately compensated by the thought that each of us, in his small way, is contributing something new and true for a better mankind.

There is one thing I am dead earnest about, and this is the cause. It is my life, my business, my religion, my hobby, my sweetheart, my wife and my mistress, my breath and my meat. I work at it in the daytime and dream of it at night. Its hold on me grows, not lessens, as time goes on. Therefore, I cannot carry on friendship or a love affair or even a conversation without relating to it – this force that drives and guides my life. I evaluate people, books, ideas, and actions according to how they affect the cause and by their attitude toward it.

I have already been in jail because of my ideals and, if necessary, I'm ready to go before the firing squad."

Jesus' disciples were not asked to affirm a statement of faith or to recite a creed. They were simply asked to follow. In following they were to set themselves apart to God and set themselves apart from the world. For your own personal application, list three obedience or consecration issues you dealt with in the last month.

This letter points out the need of authority in our lives. The revolutionary says, "I evaluate people, books, ideas, and actions according to how they affect the cause and by their attitude toward it." He is making a case for the role of authority in his life. For him, his source of authority was the tenets of the cause. Everything and everyone passed through a filter in his mind as to how they stood in comparison with these beliefs.

What is the source of authority for a disciple? What filter does she/he use to determine her/his belief system and actions? If we are truly to be consecrated, we must be sure of our authority base. There are two sources of authority in a believer's life:

The Bible, The Written Word

The Bible is by its nature an objective authority. Skill is needed to handle the text in a logical way, taking into account the occasion of the original writers and readers. This means we go from the "there and then" of the passage to the "here and now" of our lives. This will be discussed at greater length in Lesson 10.

Jesus, The Living Word

Jesus' voice to us is a subjective authority. The skill needed is the ability to discern the voice of the Lord from all other voices.

Note, you will never find the Living Word saying anything contrary to the Written Word. Often listening to the Living Word helps us apply the injunctions from the written word. Together the living and written word build a base of authority that creates a grid or filter through which a believer screens everything in their life pertaining to belief and behavior.

IMPARTATION: He Gave Himself Away

In the last section we found consecration/obedience is a motivation for living a discipling lifestyle. In this section we find love is also a motivation in discipleship. Love was, and always is the standard by which discipleship is judged. But it's not the kind of love that is often portrayed in Hollywood. It's Calvary love – love that leads to service and the laying down of one's life.

- Do you know what love is?
- Do you know how to love?
- Are you a loving person?

These three questions, thought distinct, are all quite crucial and require a response from every believer. Let us deal with each question in turn.

A. Do you know what love is?

This question seems more appropriately relegated to the domain of poets. However, in a world where we can say in the same breath,

"I love my fiancée," and "I love hamburgers," some defining of the concept of love is necessary.

There are at least four components to the love experience. These are not four different kinds of love, but four essential components of love.

There is love we **feel**. This can be emotion or physical touch. It is expressed through kind words and expressions of affection. We have words like "erotic" that are descriptive of this component of love. Erotic has a negative connotation in our society due to the abuse of this component of love, but when expressed in a God-ordained manner, it is a celebration.

There is love we **share**. This is love reflecting give and take. It has an ebb and flow nature to it. This is the love of friends. This component of love demands reciprocity to be operative. We have words like "Philadelphia" that means the city of "brotherly love."

There is love we **know**. The appropriate way to love another person needs to be defined for us, i.e. we love our mother in ways different from our coach or our boyfriend. For a believer, the appropriate way to love others is defined for us by God in the Bible and through the example of Jesus. We also receive definitions for appropriate ways to love from our culture. Ultimately, for love to make sense, we must know and abide by the God-given principles.

There is love we **give**. This is love coming from an act of the will. It has a clear purpose and is direct in nature. Here, our behavior is reflective of a rational act of the will. Whereas, sharing is give-and-receive, "giving" love is one directional. It goes from you to someone else who is in need of your expression of love. Loving your enemy would be a radical expression of giving love.

These four components of love (feeling, sharing, knowing, and giving) act in collaboration with one another. It is probably not possible to express one component without the others being involved to some degree. However, they must take priority over one another given differing situations. When we allow what we feel to dominate, it is quite easy for our behavior to be modified by our feelings. This may lead to impulsive behavior, and is often an ineffective way to live.

On the other hand, when we take the time to know the biblical mandates for proper love expressions and then act in accordance with them we will discover our behavior is modified by what is godly.

When the New Testament writers searched for a word to describe the love of God for a fallen world, they used the Greek word *Agape.* Agape reflects the component of love that we give. It was a decision of God the Father to give His Son for us. Just as Paul tells us, "God has poured out his love into our hearts by the Holy Spirit, whom he has given us. You see, at just the right time, when we were still powerless, Christ died for the ungodly.... While we were still sinners, Christ died for us." Romans 5:5-8

B. Do you know how to love?

The love of God is His selfless, purposeful, and willful giving of Himself. For us to know how to love, it must involve us in the same expression of selfless giving of ourselves to God, other believers, and the pre-Christians around us. Jesus is the perfect model of loving, thus His ways of loving deserve our careful attention.

Take some time now and examine Jesus' first sermon in Luke 4:18-19 (also see Isaiah 61:1-2) and identify the specific ways Jesus showed His love. Write out a list and discuss. Having a warm and tender heart or thinking lovely thoughts did not bring relief to these mentioned in these passages. Love is demonstrated to those in need. Jesus knew He was the one who was to be the "ransom for many." He knew who He was and what He was to do.

It's the same for us. We are new creatures in Christ Jesus; we have new identities. He has told us what to do: "This is how we know what love is: Christ gave his life for us. We too, then, ought to give our lives for our brothers! If anyone has material possessions and sees his brother in need but has no pity on him, how can he claim that he has the love of God in his heart? Dear children! Our love should not be just words and talk; it must be true love, which shows itself in action." 1 John 3:16-18

Here are some suggestions on knowing how to love more effectively:

1. Make relationships a priority.

If you want transformative friendships, you must give them a high priority. You cannot assume love will "just happen." You must be careful to schedule time with your friends. If friendship really is a high priority, it will become regularly visible in you weekly calendar.

2. Don't play it safe.

Love is a risk demonstrated through transparency and vulnerability. Transparency says something is clear enough to be seen through without anything inhibiting full visibility. Vulnerability means someone is capable of being wounded.

Without transparency and vulnerability, relationships remain at the surface level. If you are to love as Christ loved, you must live just as risky as He did. When you block yourself off from others, you will find yourself in emotional, spiritual, and eventually even physical difficulties. God intended for us to be known – known by the Father and by His community.

3. Create warmth in your friendships.

We are a society terribly out of touch with each other. So look people in the eyes when talking, touch them, and practice smiling until it becomes comfortable. Share your feelings and not just your ideas. Actively listen in conversations.

4. Affirm your friends.

When we meet a person and see only a problem, we imprison the person in their problem. We need to see our friends, through faith, as Jesus sees them: unique, worthwhile, with infinite possibilities. In doing so we call forth a new being. Let's speak the truth in love to one another, especially the good and affirming truth.

I love Cervantes' story of Don Quixote. In the musical rendition of this story, *Man of LaMancha*, we see an aging Don Quixote. Those around him think him to be quite odd. He determined to go on a grand quest. He views himself as a royal knight out to do right and create justice in the world. He pursues this dream despite the fact the age of knights and chivalry has long since passed.

He comes upon a stubby, chubby man named Sancho Panza. He asks Sancho to travel with him and be his "royal squire" and participate in his quest. Sancho is intrigued by Quixote and figures he has nothing to lose, so he joins him on his travels.

They come to a rustic inn. The innkeeper goes out to meet this comical couple. Quixote asks permission to come and lodge with him in his "great manor." Now this innkeeper is willing to take payment from anyone, even from loony tunes like these two. Within the inn is a servant girl. She does more than serve meals. She also provides late night entertainment for many of the male guests. In the musical, Quixote sings a song to her changing her name from Aldonza, the kitchen wench, to Dulcinea, the pure chaste woman – the epitome a good man's dreams. She calls him crazy, for surely he doesn't know who she is, and what she does.

At the end of the story, Don Quixote receives a head injury and is on his deathbed. But as he comes back to his senses, he starts to leave his fanciful notions of quest behind. Probably one of the most moving moments occurs around his bed. Sancho, the innkeeper, and Aldonza all gather around to comfort him in his condition, and as they do so they beg him not to change. For Don Quixote had touched them with the power of affirmation, and in doing so had released them from the despair of their meager lives and called them to dream for what they wished they could become. Somehow this odd, old man had touched the deepest aspirations of everyone he met, and they loved him for it.

So too, when we see a person as Jesus sees them. When we truthfully affirm what we see, a new being begins to emerge by the transforming power of Jesus. Be a Don Quixote!

5. Be real

In Paul's letter to the Corinthians he addresses the way they had been abusing their relationships with each other within the Christian community. Paul uses the human body as an illustration and draws attention to two separate and opposite attitudes that occur in a body of believers. Paul affirms neither of these attitudes.

He tells them anyone who feels inferior to other members of the body fails to understand what God has done for them. The grace of God has made them new in Christ and coheirs with all the saints. Paul also declares there are some who have superior attitudes toward other members in the body. This too misses what God has done. These think too highly of themselves - higher than they out to think. So high that they had come to disregard other members of the body for whom Christ has died.

A **real** person is someone who avoids both extremes. They have a real picture of who they are in relationship to Jesus. They are overjoyed at God's grace in their life. They recognize this same grace has set them and their brothers and sisters in Christ free. Paul uses these words to describe a real person in Christ: "For by the grace given me I say to every one of you: Do not think of yourself more highly than you ought, but rather think of yourself with sober judgment, in accordance with the measure of faith God has given you." Romans 12:3

Take a little break from the normal routine of this class and read the first chapter from Margery Williams', *The Velveteen Rabbit.* Jesus knew some truths are best communicated in story and here's a chance to try out his method. Read the first chapter aloud as you would read a bedtime story to a child. It's a great story of a stuffed velveteen rabbit being made "real" by a little boy's love.

C. Are you a loving person?

Are you a lover or a taker? That is a scary question we must all face many times in our lives. The issue goes beyond feeling good about God's love, or even knowing how Jesus loved. The bottom line question is, "Are you actively loving as Jesus loved?"

How do you get there? Again a quote from Coleman:

> "How else could they ever fulfill the commission for their Lord with joy and inward peace? They needed an expression of Christ so real that their lives would be filled with His presence. Evangelism had to be a burning compulsion within them purifying their desires and guiding their thoughts. Nothing less than a personal baptism of the Holy Spirit would suffice. The super-human work to which they were called demanded supernatural help – an endowment of power from on High."

The Master Plan of Evangelism 69

As we discussed in lesson one, Jesus not only laid out His purpose and program for discipleship to the Twelve, but He also promised His continual presence and the provision of the Spirit's filling. We are called to love as God does. To do so, we must be filled with Him.

DELEGATION: He Gave Them Work

"Of course *your* sheepdog can't do that. But when's the last time you spent any real quality time with him?"

Jesus trained His disciples. He equipped them to take over the mission of spreading the message and power of the gospel everywhere. To learn how to do this they must learn how to do a few smaller things first. Would they understand, would they be faithful and responsible, and would they grow from their experiences? The best way to be sure this is done is to give practical work assignments and empower a protégé to be carried out. Here is a simple guideline to show how Jesus discipled the Twelve.

Biblical Reference	Principle	Illustration
Mark 1 and 2	Model	You do it, he/she watches.
Mark 3:13-15	Mentor	You do it, he/she helps.
Mark 6:7-13	Monitor	He/she does it, you help.
Mark 16:15-18	Motivate	He/she does it, you watch.
Acts 6:1-7; 2 Timothy 2:2	Multiply	He/she does it, someone else watches.

Before Jesus sent them out in pairs He demonstrated how to minister as they watched on. He then helped them. In this action Jesus demonstrated the Kingdom work is to be experienced in companionship. It is the work of friends. When working together with the power of the Holy Spirit, we can face anything.

"His method was to get the disciples into vital experience with God, and to show them how He worked, before telling them they had to do it." *The Master Plan of Evangelism 82*

Lesson 4

The Master's Method III: Supervision & Reproduction

We come now to the conclusion of our study of the components of Jesus' discipling methodology as discussed in Robert Coleman's book, *The Master Plan of Evangelism.* In this lesson we focus on his final two components: supervision and reproduction.

Supervision: He Held Them Accountable

To quickly summarize where we have been thus far in this book:

- We watched Jesus carefully select faithful individuals to be with Him.
- He repeatedly emphasized to them the need for commitment to bring in the Kingdom of God.
- He demonstrated the power of conquering love.
- He assigned practical tasks to His disciples so they would develop Kingdom ministry skills.

Now Jesus wants to see what they've learned. Jesus expects His disciples to grow in their understanding of the nature of God, the sinfulness of man, and a host of other truths through the things they were doing. He was not just trying to teach them a few tasks to do for Him after He left for the right hand of God. Jesus has one primary goal in mind – the salvation of the world. If this goal is to be reached, His disciples must keep their focus and not settle for minor victories.

Supervision occurs when a disciple is held responsible or accountable for the things entrusted to him. Accountability is a part of our daily lives. Banks expect us to be responsible for the amount of funds we have in our checking accounts. Professors require we read the syllabus and complete assignments on time. Our friends assume that we will act friendly to them, and so on.

A. Jesus' rationale for holding disciples accountable:

First, Jesus intended to use the tasks the disciples were given to teach them practical applications for their personal lives. "When he was alone, the Twelve and the others around him asked him about the parables.... 'Consider carefully what you hear'...'Whoever has will be given more; whoever does not have, even what he has will be taken from him.'" (Mark 4:10, 24, 25)

Second, after the disciples were sent out, they were expected to return to share their experience with the group. "When the apostles returned, they reported to Jesus what they had done." (Luke 9:10)

Third, during these sharing times with the disciples, Jesus would caution them against taking excessive pride in their accomplishments. "However, do not rejoice that the spirits submit to you, but rejoice that your names are written in heaven." (Luke 10:20)

Lastly, Jesus wanted the disciples to receive the rest they needed in body and soul from all their labors. "Then, because so many people were coming and going that they did not even have a chance to eat, he said to them, 'Come with me by yourselves to a quiet place and get some rest.'" (Mark 6:31)

B. In God's Family, Accountability is Mutual

"I accept the fact that you feel I should stay off the couch. But I might also point out that you just left the toilet seat up."

Accountability, within most people's minds, conjures up a lion tamer barking orders to a caged animal. Thus, accountability is something to be avoided because it sounds like punishment. Or it sounds like a large corporation with ever descending levels of authoritarian bosses. Does accountability mean submission to somebody in the body of Christ who becomes the vehicle of God's will over your life? To answer this let's consider the Biblical concept of mutual accountability.

Mutual accountability is a concept made manifest, first, by Jesus Christ. Christianity is unique. When Jesus came into this world, He brought into being a new approach to functional relationships between people. In the "Gentile world," as Jesus called it, mutual accountability was not practiced. People operated primarily out of selfish motives having little or no interest in helping others reach their goals – except when it might benefit their self-interest. (Mark 10:42-45)

Nevertheless, the apostle Paul made it clear accountability to other Christians is essential for personal Christian growth. The guidelines for mutual accountability are rooted in the authority of Jesus and His Word. Again, as we have mentioned before, to be a disciple means we are "people of the Book." There are many examples of mutually responsible relationships in the Bible. Here is a list of a few with references:

- Elders to regular members in Christ's body - 1 Peter 5:2,3
- Christians in general to elders – 1 Timothy 5:7-20; Hebrews 13:17

- Younger individuals to older individuals – 1 Peter 5:5,6
- Husbands to wives – Ephesians 5:25,28; Colossians 3:19; 1 Peter 3:7; 1 Corinthians 7:3,4
- Wives to husbands – Ephesians 5:22,24; Colossians 3:18; Titus 2:3-5; 1 Peter 3:1-4
- Parents to children – Ephesians 6:4; Colossians 3:21
- Children to parents – Ephesians 6:1-3; Colossians 3:20
- Masters (employers) to slaves (employees) – Ephesians 6:9; Colossians 4:1
- Slaves of Masters – Ephesians 6:5-8; 1 Peter 2:18,19
- Christians to governmental officials – Romans 13:1,5,7; 1 Peter 2:13-17

As you can see, accountability here listed is a two-way street. One party does not dominate over the other, even though the function or role may be distinctive. On the contrary, it seems these relationships underscore each party involved has a vested interest. It doesn't point out dominance as much as it points out each one being responsible. People are neither solely independent nor dependent, but interdependent (mutually).

C. Basic principles concerning authority and accountability.

Christian leaders are a gift to us from God (Ephesians 4:11-13), and we need to nurture and enhance in every way possible our relationship with those responsible to us. Being accountable to a leader does not mean you give up your responsibility over your decisions. We will have no one but ourselves to appeal to or blame when we stand before the judgment seat of Christ. A leader should never be followed if their counsel contradicts the Word of God or gives you permission to sin.

We must learn to be responsible *to* others rather than responsible *for* others. *"Responsible for"* means we assume the responsibility for another's actions, which is never the case. Being *"responsible to"* means we serve another by pointing in the right direction, but we never assume blame or credit for another's decisions or actions.

"Hey, wait just a minute! Who's the guy with the pipe?"

Being accountable to a leader does not mean "blind obedience." There is an erroneous line of thinking that recognizes the Lordship of Jesus and his headship over the body of Christ. However, it further views Christian leaders as extensions of Jesus' authority on earth. As this reasoning continues, these leaders then speak with the authority of Jesus to believers under their care. Therefore, believers are to take their counsel with the same authority in their personal lives as unto the Lord. They are asked to submit all major decisions to their leader. The dominating leader is to pray and receive a "peace from the Lord" or to receive a "check from the Lord" on any given decision. Obedience to these judgments is viewed as giving obedience directly to the Lord Jesus. Thus, the believer gives up full responsibility over their decisions to a leader of their local Christian group. This view assumes too much authority for a leader and it is not consistent with biblical revelation.

This line of thinking creates a continuum with blind obedience on the opposite end from living completely autonomously. The autonomous person, in relation to leadership and authority, does not allow anyone to have a voice in the decisions and choices they face. This individualism does not reflect the biblical example either.

Rather than blind obedience or total independence, Scripture affirms relationships of mutual accountability where each one earnestly attempts to love in a selfless manner and each one attempts to be submissive and give deference to the other. This fosters neither the sick dependence of blind obedience, nor the offensive independence of the autonomous person, but the interdependence of those who live with mutual concern for one another.

D. The following questions will serve as a self-test to help you to get in touch with your attitudes and feelings toward authority figures in the body of Christ.

- How do I view the people in my church who are in positions of leadership? Do I feel more or less important than they? Do I respond and honor them as fellow members of Christ's body, or do I judge them negatively?
- Do I ever share my inner life and struggles with others, or do I keep my insecurities to myself?
- How do I react when a Christian friend disagrees with me? Am I threatened? Do I try to defend myself? Do I insist on doing things my own way?
- Do I avoid situations where a Christian friend or leader might question my actions or attitudes?
- How often have I admitted to others I have been wrong? Do I always have to be right to feel at ease?
- Do I hold my Christian friends to their commitments to God, to me, to other Christian friends, and to pre-Christians?

E. Why accountability is necessary in discipling relationships.

- Mutual accountability provides encouragement to a disciple who does not meet with immediate "success" or up to his/her self-imposed expectations.
- Mutual accountability helps to prevent excessive pride in personal accomplishments from clouding the essential truth - that of receiving God's grace and recognizing we are but saved sinners.
- We all need to continually review the really important things, and to embed them firmly into our lives, and to rekindle the vision they are attempting to achieve.

- Jesus intends to push us through the first-fruits of ministry (immediate enthusiasm, zeal, joy) to full maturity.
- Mutual accountability prevents us from becoming a slacker. "The sluggard craves and gets nothing, but the desires of the diligent are fully satisfied." (Proverbs 13:4. Also see Proverbs 20:4; 26:16)
- Mutual accountability helps a disciple discover potential problems before they grow to dimensions too large to restore.

F. We are called by God to live covenant-making lives

The concept of covenant is, for the most part, a foreign idea in our modern era, but it is foundational for understanding functional relationships in the ancient Near East. This was especially true at the time of Abraham.

A prominent covenant form from this time period occurred between a conquering king and the vanquished vassal lord. A series of blessings (having your borders protected by the king) and curses (punishments if you failed to keep the covenant) would be issued. The vassal would pledge his allegiance to the conquering king at a special ceremony where the blessings and curses are read publicly.

The word covenant literally means "to cut." A cutting ceremony would seal the covenant. An animal, like a ram, bull, or maybe a dove, would be cut in two pieces. The pieces would be pulled apart and the vassal lord would be asked to walk among the pieces forming a figure eight. This would be done in the presence of the conquering king. Symbolically it said, "This is what will happen to the vassal, should he break the covenant. The king would walk among the pieces of the vassal." Certainly a vivid picture and the meaning is not lost on anyone.

With this background, we find an interesting episode in the life of Abraham in Genesis 15. God, the Sovereign, comes to Abram and pledges to bless him with a lineage as vast as the stars of the sky. Abram believed God, and his belief is counted as righteousness. The Lord gives instructions for Abram to prepare for a ceremony. Abram was to bring a heifer, a goat, and a ram. He cut them into two pieces and arranged the halves opposite each other. As evening approached, God put Abram into a deep sleep. A smoking firepot appeared and moved among the pieces. The fire represents God, the Sovereign. Only here, the Sovereign, rather than the vassal, passes among the pieces, and seals this covenant with the pledge of His own "body". God pledges Himself to this covenant.

Today, we see what Abram could not see. This covenant is repeatedly broken by the unfaithful nations of Israel and Judah. Many prophets implore the people to return in fidelity to their Sovereign God. Due to their unfaithfulness, they deserved judgment. Astonishingly, God remained true to His covenant. He did so by sending His Son in human form to have his body laid open on a cross to fulfill this covenant. Our covenant-keeping God reestablishes a new covenant. He saves out of this world a people for Him.

Covenant relationships are very important to God. Growing to become people who live as covenant making and keeping people is a call of God on our lives. It is not any more or less difficult to live in covenant with God today as it was for Abram. We discover mutually accountable relationships are a great source of blessing and help us to remain faithful to God and each other.

REPRODUCTION: The Evidence of a Trained Disciple

As Coleman points out from Jesus' illustration of the vine and the branches, the purpose of every disciple is to bear fruit. If His indwelling Spirit truly grafts us into the very life of Christ, then we should expect to see results. "A barren Christian is a contradiction. A tree is known by its fruit." *The Master Plan of Evangelism 107*

The fruitfulness of our lives is not measured by our level of talents, but by the perpetuation of the life of Christ in and through us in a desperate world. Again, we must remember our focus. Not haphazard patches on a sick world – a frantic blur of activity for the sake of the kingdom, but a carefully considered life that takes a younger believer and passes on everything necessary for life and godliness.

"What really counts in the ultimate perpetuation of our work is the faithfulness with which our converts go out and make leaders out of their converts, not simply more followers... The test of any work of evangelism thus is not what is seen at the moment...but in the effectiveness with which the work continues in the next generation." *The Master Plan of Evangelism 110*

"There is no use to pray for the world. What good would it do? God already loves them and has given His Son to save them. No, there is no use to pray vaguely for the world. The world is lost and blind in sin. The only hope for the world is for individuals to go to them with the Gospel of Salvation, and having won them to the Savior, not to leave them but to work with them faithfully, patiently, painstakingly, until they become fruitful Christians savoring the world about them with the Redeemer's love." *The Master Plan of Evangelism 109*

So, it is true that disciplers should have "spiritual grandchildren." Remember, we are affecting the next generation beyond the disciple we are discipling. Take care how you invest in another person's life. Make sure all your goals and methods are all transgenerational. Later in this book we shall learn more about transgenerational methods. Set in your heart today to establish transgenerational goals for your service for Jesus for the remainder of your life — till He comes!

A Summary of the Discipling Method of Jesus

The Model	The Principle	The Application
Acts 1:1 "Began to do" – Jesus was a living model of what He desires His disciples to be.	Discipleship is being a MODEL.	A discipler must focus on the *development of godly character qualities* in the new disciple.
Acts 1:1 "Began to teach" – Beyond modeling, Jesus taught truth by instruction.	Discipleship entails TEACHING the revelation of Jesus.	A discipler must focus on the skill of *Bible study* with the new disciple.
Mark 3:14 "That they should be with Him" – Jesus made himself available for close personal association.	Discipleship is a_ RELATIONSHIP, not a PRESET PROGRAM.	A discipler must work toward the *development of true fellowship* between the new disciple and the family of God.
Mark 6:7 "He sent them out two-by-two" – Jesus began a process that continues today.	Discipleship is a TRANSGENERATIONAL PROCESS involving EVANGELISM and TEACHING (Deut. 6:1,2)	The discipler must equip the new disciple in *evangelism and the ability to disciple.* (2 Tim 2:2)

The Model	The Principle	The Application
Mark 6:30 "The apostles gathered around Jesus and reported to him all they had done and taught."	Discipleship entails MUTUAL ACCOUNTABILITY to the commands of Jesus and our ministry to Him.	The discipler must model *mutual sharing and support* while remaining *encouraging* and *assertive.* (Gal 6:2; Eph 5:21)
Matthew 4:19 "Come, follow me and I will make you fishers of people."	Discipleship is SKILLS DEVELOPMENT.	The discipler must build in the new disciple the *necessary skills* (prayer, worship, teaching, etc.)

© Brady Bobbink

Lesson 5

Discipleship Demands Leadership and Dedication

"We seem not to live long enough to take our lives seriously."
— George Bernard Shaw

Living Wisely

No one can say we are not busy people. We fill our lives with activity and flurry, so much so that phrases such as "no time today," "I'm really busy," "Boy, I'm tired," and "maybe later" seem ubiquitous to our vocabulary.

Now, being busy is no sin. But the tragedy trapping so many of us is we have such a fuzzy, nebulous understanding of why we're going so hard (let alone knowing where all this hustle and bustle is taking us). It is a sad commentary when a person can live his entire life, and can point to many accomplishments, but still don't have the slightest idea why he lived as he did.

One consequence of our high tech society is a lamentable loss in meaning to life and human dignity. We feel of little value, and we suspect we will have little impact on our world. For, "who am I against such large problems in such an immense world?"

What is even more tragic is seeing Christians who have the "upward call in Christ Jesus", who are urged "to live a life worthy of the calling you have received", living such shallow lives and totally caught up in a race to nowhere.

Paul cautions us, "Be very careful, then, how you live – not as unwise but as wise, making the most of every opportunity, because the days are evil" — Ephesians 5:15, 16

Living wisely and dreaming go hand-in-hand. We must become visionaries! We need to establish for ourselves biblical purposes (what we are to be), and from these purpose statements build Godly goals (what we are to do), and then see our priorities (the way our lives are actually lived out) reflect these purposes and goals.

Having dreamed, we become steadfastly dedicated to these Christ-centered directions. It is only through dedication and commitment to the purposes and plans of Christ that our life will find real and lasting significance.

Some Distinctive Characteristics of a Dedicated Life

- Essential characteristics of the dedicated person include idealism, zeal, devotion, and the willingness to sacrifice to achieve ideals. Not only is it important to have dreams worth living for, but we also need a cause worth sacrificing for.
- Dedication is contagious. Associating with a dedicated person will breed dedication in you.
- Being dedicated sets you apart from the rest of the world. Decide to be a person who gives 100% in a world who gives 50%.
- A dedicated person does not fear making mistakes as much as they fear making the same mistake again. A wise person learns from his/her mistakes.
- "if you make mean little demands upon people, you will get a mean little response which is all you deserve, but, if you make big demands on them, you will get a heroic response… work on the assumption that if you call for big sacrifices people will respond to this and, moreover, the relatively smaller sacrifices will come quite naturally." Douglas Hyde, *Dedication and Leadership 18*
- The dedicated person will postpone immediate satisfaction or gratification for achieving more important long-range goals.

Distinguishing Marks of Discipling Leadership

A leader is an agent for change who gets things done. Often we think of leaders as aggressive activists, people who are bold in personality, articulate in speech and pleasant in appearance. We often assume leaders are born. While these characteristics can be very helpful for leadership, an essential characteristic for leadership is a person who sees a need, develops a goal, and puts a plan into motion toward that goal. This describes a discipler: a person with Godly vision coupled with faith who takes action. The following characteristics underscore the distinguishing marks of discipling leadership:

- The process of making a person into a leader is the development of an integrated person. These are "ones who understand what they believe, are deeply dedicated to it, and who try unceasingly to relate their beliefs to every facet of their own lives and to the society in which they live." Douglas Hyde, *Dedication and Leadership 157*
- Leadership is learned.
- A discipling leader is a thermostat rather than a thermometer. They bring influence to their environment rather than just conforming to the climate of their environment.
- Discipling leaders are ones who strive for effectiveness in all that they do. They attempt, with all the resources within them, to become the best they can become no matter the situation, whether the best engineer, bricklayer, musician, social worker, or pastor. "Best" needs to be defined. First, it must be seen as the best we can do realistically evaluating our resources of time, money, energy, expertise, and gifting. Then we must determine what expenditure of resources we can give. Given this specific situation we do our best.

The Cost of Leadership

"No one need aspire to leadership in the work of God who is not prepared to pay a price greater than his contemporaries and colleagues are willing to pay. True leadership always exacts a heavy toll on the whole man, and the more effective the leadership is, the higher the price to be paid." J. Oswald Sanders, *Spiritual Leadership 104*

- Self-sacrifice: A price paid every day. Paul was a supreme example of self-sacrifice. (2 Cor. 4:8-11)
- Loneliness: A discipler is a believer committed to personal growth in the Lord. A growing person often feels shoved to the head of the pack. Though he may be the friendliest of people, there are times when he will tread a lonely path. (2 Timothy 1:15)

Ever since leaving the larvae stage, Phil felt isolated from the others.

- Fatigue: The ever-increasing demands made on a discipler may drain the emotional energy and wear down the most robust person. (2 Cor. 4:15, 16)
- Criticism: No leader is exempt from criticism. His/her humility is seen most clearly in the manner in which he/she accepts or reacts to it. (1 Cor. 4:3-5)
- Time to think: A price paid by disciplers is the time taken for strategic thinking and meditation. We do not often think of this as a price to pay, but it is. Many people do not take time to really think. (Mark 6:31)

Goals that Mobilize: How to set goals and priorities that move God's people toward his purposes.

As stated in the introduction, the effective discipler is one who thinks clearly along the lines of purposes, goals and priorities. The following article by Ted Engstrom instructs how to establish "Goals that Mobilize."

Purpose or goals?

It is important for a discipler to distinguish between purposes and specific, achievable, measurable, and manageable goals. For instance, ask yourself if the following are purposes or goals:

- To glorify God through our campus ministry
- To be a mature Christian

- To teach an effective lesson in Small Group
- To be a good friend and helper
- To be a better discipler

Archery without a target gave Steve the satisfaction of knowing he would never miss. And yet the excitement soon waned.

It might surprise you to know that none of the above bullets are goals. They are all purpose statements. A purpose is something for which we ultimately hope. It is not necessarily measurable in itself, but is a clear direction toward which we wish to move.

Our purpose statements often fall in the category of things we want to be. To be mature, to be a better, to be a good – these are the ideals toward which we are striving. But it is our goals which help us determine how much progress, if any, we are making toward our "to be" purposes.

Below are examples of specific goals. I think you will readily see the difference between purposes and goals:

- To share Christ with a pre-Christian twice a week
- To spend 15 minutes in prayer each day
- To tithe a minimum of 10 percent of my income
- To eat with my discipleship group once a week
- To learn to fly and airplane by the end of the summer

Now of course no one can guarantee, for example, eating with my discipleship group once a week will make me a better discipler. But it does give me a specific, tangible means of measuring this important purpose in my life. Therefore, all of the above are measurable goals.

Communicate and Mobilize

It seems God made us to respond with enthusiasm to something worthwhile, specific, and measurable to tackle. That's because good goals are related to faith.

A goal is a statement about how we hope things are going to be at some time in the future. It is a statement of faith. Any statement about tomorrow is a statement of faith. This is an important concept. Don't miss it. As the writer in Hebrews said, "Faith is the substance of things hoped for" (Hebrews 11:1)

Goals have the power to lift our eyes from the mud below to the sky above. They are a statement about what could be, what should be, or what can be. Notice goals are not statements about what will be. That is in God's hands. But they are statements about what we believe God wants us to do or to be, in light of his word.

Well-written Goals

Many may be asking at this moment, how do I write goal statements? I know what we hope to be as a campus ministry, but how do we develop the goals that help us measure our progress toward what we want to be? Below are some statements that might help you.

Well-written goals are:

- Stated in terms of end results
- Achievable in a time span
- Definite as to what is expected
- Practical and feasible
- Precisely stated in terms of quantities, where applicable
- Limited to one important goal statement

Poorly written goals tend to be:

- Stated in terms of process or activities
- Are never fully achievable; no specific target dates
- Ambiguous as to what is expected
- Theoretical or idealistic
- Too brief and indefinite, or too long and complex
- Written with two or more goals per statement

Goals may cover different time periods. You may have immediate goals for this week, month and year. Then you may have short-range goals for the next two or three years. Finally you may have long-range goals for five years or more. Another way of looking at the characteristics of good goals is to use the following items as a checklist of questions to ask for any goal statements you have developed:

- Is this goal accomplishable: do you believe you can do it (under God's leading)?
- Docs this goal havc a date: will you know when you want to do it?
- Is this goal measurable: will you know that it has in fact happened?
- Does this goal have steps (a plan): do you know how to reach it?
- Is this goal claimed: do you know who will be responsible for the following the plan?
- Is this goal supported: do we have the resources to accomplish it?

The ABC's of Prioritizing

Now after you have set your goals, you may still have confusion and misunderstanding in the group if you do not prioritize them. Especially with the limited manpower, time, and financial resources, it is important for us to determine the top items requiring our best efforts. Here is a little prioritizing system to help you sort out the most important items. It is simply called the ABC technique.

Start by making a list of all the goals you have considered. There is no reason why we have one goal as our top priority. We are more likely to have a number of goals, all of which we consider very important. There is a simple and effective way of sorting this out in terms of priorities. Instead of trying to assign each goal a ranking number, assign it a value, an A, B, or C.

- A – "Must do" or very high value
- B – "Should do" or medium value
- C – "Can do" or low value

You can use the ABC technique in one of two ways. The first way is to go down your list and decide which of these goals you consider to be A goals. If it's a B or a C go right past it. Just mark the A's. Now go back to the list and decide which ones are C goals, low priority. The rest are automatically B's. A second way is to pause at each goal and decide whether you think it is an A, B, or C. It does not matter which of these methods you use. Some people find one easier than the other. Remember, goals for which you have no priorities are useless.

Goals and Leadership

It isn't always easy to put flesh and bones on the exalted purposes God has called us to in his Word. But developing achievable goals for these purposes and prioritizing them can be one of the most practical and measurable means of mobilizing believers to truly seek his kingdom and his righteousness.

Freedom was taken with this article to adapt it to a campus ministry setting. It first appeared in *Pastoral Renewal*, October 1980, Vol. 1, #4

Lesson 6

The Disciplines of Discipleship

Discipline is training that amends, molds, and sharpens the mental abilities and moral character of a person. Often our first thought is of punishment when we consider discipline. Good correction helps a person who lacks of self-control to stand upright again (trusting that this direct attention will aid in the development of self-control). Thus, to discipline simply means to impose order upon disorder within the mind, heart and spirit.

Spiritual disciplines are training tools for the spiritually unruly. They foster growth in the knowledge of God, escalation in spiritual development, and progress in living an effective Christian lifestyle. The disciplines enable the "fruit of the Spirit" to bear a bountiful harvest in our lives, bringing love, joy, peace, patience, kindness, goodness, faithfulness, gentleness and self-control.

> "Superficiality is the curse of our age. The doctrine of instant satisfaction is a primary spiritual problem. The desperate need today is not for a greater number of intelligent people, or gifted people. But for deep people...
>
> Neither should we think of the spiritual disciplines as some dull drudgery aimed at exterminating laughter from the face of the earth. Joy is the keynote of all disciplines. The purpose of the disciplines is liberation from the stifling

slavery to self-interest and fear... Singing, dancing, even shouting characterize the disciplines of the spiritual life...

Our ordinary method of dealing with ingrained sin is to launch a frontal attack. We rely on our willpower and determination...we determine never to do it again; we pray against it, fight against it, set our will against it. But it is all in vain, and we find ourselves once again morally bankrupt or, worse yet, so proud of our external righteousness that "whitened sepulchers" is a mild description of our condition...

Willpower will never succeed in dealing with the deeply ingrained habits of sin.... Willpower has no defense against the careless word, the unguarded moment. The will has the same deficiency as the Law – it can deal only with externals. It is not sufficient to bring about the necessary transformation of the inner spirit.

The needed change within us is God's work, not ours. The demand is for an inside job, and only God can work from the inside.

Our world is hungry for genuinely changed people. Leo Tolstoy observed, 'Everybody thinks of changing humanity and nobody thinks of changing himself.' Let us be among those who believe that the inner transformation of our lives is a goal worthy of our best effort." Excerpts from: Richard J. Foster, *Celebration of Discipline 1-9*

Review this Sampling from King Solomon Concerning Discipline

- "The fear of the Lord is the beginning of knowledge, but fools despise wisdom and discipline." Proverbs 1:7
- "My son, do not despise the Lord's discipline and do not resent his rebuke, because the Lord disciplines those he loves, as a father the son he delights in." Proverbs 3:11, 12
- "At the end of your life you will groan, when your flesh and body are spent. You will say, 'How I hated disciplines! How my heart spurned correction! I would not obey my teachers or listen to my instructors. I have to come to the brink of utter ruin in the midst of the whole assembly." Proverbs 5:11-14

- "He who heeds discipline shows the way to life, but whoever ignores correction leads other astray." Proverbs 10:17
- "Whoever loves discipline loves knowledge, but he who hates correction is stupid." Proverbs 12:1
- He who ignores discipline despiscs himself, but whoever heeds correction gains understanding." Proverbs 15:32
- Also see Proverbs 1:2, 3, 5:21-23; 6:20-23; 9:13-18; 13:18, 24; 15:5-10.

In what ways do you resonant with Solomon's observations? Share these thoughts back-and-forth with a friend or small group.

Impediments to a Disciplined Life

A. Our age of relativism encourages an undisciplined approach to life.

New Age stop signs.

The dominant worldview in America assumes nothing is universally right or wrong; nothing intrinsically good or bad. Good and evil are not built in, essential, unchangeable qualities of life; they are only descriptions of our perceptions in different situations. Everyone is really "free" to think, live and love as they feel best. Therefore, there is no standard to which we should aspire, other than the "standard" within each of us.

B. The over-spiritualization of spontaneity

In some Christian circles things planned or scheduled are often seen as less "Spirit-led". Strategy for ministry and mission is viewed with suspicion. The "flesh" must be in control. Only those activities of the Spirit that occur on the spur of the moment or are received by special revelation carry ultimate spiritual weight. This is not to say that special revelation is in any way to be undercut, on the contrary, we are enormously blessed when the Holy Spirit works among us in this manner. But over-spiritualization occurs when we exclusively cling only to the special word. This misses the truth that faithful commitment over time produces much fruit. Often "spiritual spontaneity" is only a mask for spiritual irresponsibility and immaturity.

C. Subscribing to a sacred-secular dichotomy.

We tend to divide our lives into things with spiritual value and the remainder is non-spiritual. This flies in the face of a true understanding of spirituality. Our Christian faith is integrated into every fabric of our normal lives. Moreover, this is precisely the essential task of discipleship, to lead disciples into a comprehensive understanding of how a relationship with Jesus relates to every fiber and sector of our lives.

D. A failure to learn skills for spiritual maturity.

In many cases the normal Christian life becomes as lackadaisical and haphazard as modern secular society. Discipline is a gain-through-pain enterprise, and we tend to avoid suffering at any cost. Often suffering is equated with evil itself. Rather, it is the responsibility of the local church and the nuclear family to train young believers in righteousness.

Four Foundational Truths Concerning the Spiritual Disciplines

A. Spiritual disciplines are not an end, but a means to a greater end.

The goal is not to be recognized as a great person of prayer but to know God more deeply. The goal is not to see how rigid a life we can live but to become effective for the God's kingdom in our daily lives. "I can't see the forest for the trees." This is what happens often to disciples. They focus so much on the immediate issue of "I didn't pray today," to the exclusion of seeing the larger picture of a God who wants to be in relationship with me, and wants me to know Him.

B. Discipline brings healing into our broken lives.

Just as the beauty of God's universe is an outgrowth of God speaking order into the primeval chaos, so order coming into our disorderly lives will bring health and beauty. Unchecked anger brings hurt, but anger brought under the Spirit's control will produce understanding, forgiveness, and healing.

C. The flipside of loving compassion is careful discipline.

The writer of Hebrews 12:5-13 quotes Solomon, and reminds us that God the Father disciplines every child that He loves. Maturity and proper self-understanding only come by way of this type of loving discipline. To not act with discipline toward someone straying way off the narrow path is most unloving on our part. Remember, when the Lord Jesus commands we follow Him, His words bring blessing and curse at the same moment. Blessing for those who respond to His love, and destruction to those who reject His offer.

D. Blessing comes to the disciplined.

"No discipline seems pleasant at the time, but painful. Later on, however, it produces a harvest of righteousness and peace for those who have been trained by it." (Hebrews 12:11)

The Disciplines for your Material Resources

1. Finances

Tithes: It is an Old Testament principle for 1/10 of our income to belong to the Lord and be given at the "storehouse." A storehouse is where you are experiencing daily Christian community, where you are taught the Word of God, where you worship, where you minister to other members of Christ's body, and where you are held accountable for the faith within you. The New Testament expands the principle saying all belongs to the Lord. A beginning place is start with giving 1/10, and then increase as the Lord directs.

Offerings: Offerings are financial giving beyond our regular tithes. Whereas tithes should go to your immediate spiritual community, offerings may go to Kingdom priorities outside the local community, like missions or benevolence assistance.

2. Hospitality

"How are we supposed to make new friends if every time I invite someone over you pour boiling oil on them?"

Hospitality is using your home, for example, as a place to provide fellowship for guests. It is a strong theme throughout the Old Testament and central to the life of Jesus.

3. Tangible Goods

The sharing and giving away of the material goods to people in need (clothes, books, gifts, foot, etc.) is demonstrating God's ownership of all things and our willingness to be a good steward of those blessings.

The Disciplines for your Relationships

Time and time again we are called in the New Testament to demonstrate love and allegiance to one another. We are consistently called to minister to those around us. All of this calls for modeling, teaching, and the doing of Christ's will.

The Discipline for your Time

It doesn't take you long as a new university student to discover you can't join everything; can't support every good cause; and you can't give of yourself to every needy person. We all face the restraints built into the law of living an effective disciplined lifestyle. Effectiveness demands choices, choices, and more choices. What you choose both now and throughout your life will determine to a significant degree, your impact in this world for Christ. The priorities of your life are most clearly seen by your use of time. If being committed to Christ is the top priority of your life, but it is nowhere reflected in your weekly schedule, then this priority is only a dream or wish and not a part of actual reality.

Christian students must discipline their use of time. So give careful thought when setting personal priorities. A typical small group discipleship leader will invest several hours per week preparing, leading, and following up on his/her small group members.

If we are committed to reach our world, we must help one another properly invest our time. Review the following chart and discuss it with your fellow small group members.

A Life-Style of Biblical Priorities **Being a Steward of my Resources**		
Priority One John 15:7-11	**Priority Two** John 15:12, 13, 15b	**Priority Three** John 15:18, 19, 21, 26, 27
A Progressive commitment to: *Jesus Christ.*	A Progressive commitment to: *the body of Christ.*	A Progressive commitment to: *the work of Christ in the world.*
This involves: *Bible study, personal worship, and prayer.*	This involves: *my family, and the larger body of Christ.*	This involves: *the evangelistic mandate and the social justice mandate.*
This demands: *time alone.*	This demands: *time to love and serve one another.*	This demands: *time to go as a servant.*
Beware of over-emphasis here and becoming a *Pharisee.*	Beware of over-emphasis here and becoming a *parasite.*	Beware of over-emphasis here and becoming too *task-oriented.*

Adapted from Discipling Ministries Seminar, Barnabus, Inc.
Used by permission, 1991.

Lesson 7

Discipleship Through Small Groups I: Purpose & Attitude

In our study of the Master's Methods, Jesus' strategy is to gather a small core of individuals around Him who He would leave behind to continue His work. He associated with them, trained them, and imparted His mission to them. Jesus' discipling focused neither in the context of the multitudes, nor to individuals. Jesus gathered a small group of individuals and discipled them. This is how He passed on His life.

Experiencing truth is a key ingredient in Jesus' educational process. He let disciples experience ministry firsthand. When we do the same, we fill the world with eager, trained, experienced leaders whom the multitudes will follow.

Recurring Historical Precedents of Discipleship Through Small Groups

Moses: An Old Testament Example.

You will find in Exodus 18 an example of discipleship in action. Moses' father-in-law Jethro said, "What you are doing is not good. You and these people who come to you will only wear yourselves out. The work is too heavy for you; you cannot handle it alone. But select capable men from all the people – men who fear God, trustworthy men who hate dishonest gain – and appoint them as officials over thousands, hundreds, fifties and tens. That will make your load lighter, because they will share it with you. If you do this and God so commands, you will be able to stand the strain, and all these people will go home satisfied."

God's wisdom comes through Jethro to Moses. It is impossible for Moses alone to care for the needs of the nation. So he breaks down the nation into smaller groups of people. In these passages we see the need for trained leaders who are morally upright. Moses could not shepherd all of Israel, and we cannot effectively disciple a large community of Christian students alone. We empower others to participate in the ministry of discipling under the direction of Jesus, the Chief Shepherd and original Discipler.

An Early Church Example from the Book of Acts

Read Acts 2:46; 5:42; and 20:20. Here you find a repeating pattern – public proclamation of the word of God and then small groups gathering in houses. The first century church gathered in the large groups but also met in small groups. The significance between Act 5 and 20 is these congregations were separated by at least 25 years, existed on different continents, one is primarily Jewish while the other is primarily Gentile, and the primary leaders were Peter and Paul. Nevertheless, the pattern of large group and small group is consistent in the early church life. You see different generations, locations, races, and leaders but the same strategy.

A Church History Example – the Wesleyan Revival

George Whitefield, the great English evangelist, credited the lasting success of John Wesley, as opposed to the dying out of his own ministry, to these very principles discussed here. Wesley invested carefully in the training of women to lead cottage prayer meetings. I think this is why you often see a Wesley House on a college campus but no Whitefield House. Wesley followed the example of Jesus and the early church in his leadership. We would be wise to follow our Lord's example and the example of leaders who have gone before us.

Which is better: Small Group Discipleship or One-to-One Discipleship?

Let's look at some of the advantages of each. Why and in what way is one model more effective than the other model?

Small Group Discipleship	One-to-One Discipleship
It is closest to the model used by Jesus and the New Testament Church	It is not as difficult as leading a small group meeting
It saves time	It enhances the opportunity to really get to know another individual
It encourages transparency among peers	It offers privacy and intimacy for personal problems
It enables friendships and relationships to grow	It enables direct and customized ministry to a person
It offers a broader base for mutual support	
It releases a group dynamic for problem solving and healing	
It helps people to recognize they are not alone in their struggles	
It involves more people in intercessory prayer and with greater fervency	

I believe the ideal model of discipleship is a combination of the two methods. I think it is best to take advantage of the strengths of both methods by fostering a discipleship built around small groups as well as the one-to-one time investment by the leader with the members outside of the group. Some students may require more personalized care than others. Newer Christians often want more one-to-one time for additional help with the basics. Also, those maturing believers, who are beginning to take on ministry responsibilities, may require more one-to-one time.

Discipleship should not build an isolated dependency on one person. Rather it should integrate people into the life of a corporate community of believers by means of committed relationships and service. Any discipleship process should reflect this strategy. Discipleship is not a protracted counseling relationship, but rather an equipping, supportive relationship involving and interacting with the surrounding community of believers in constructive ways.

The Purposes of Discipleship Small Groups (Why small groups?)

Some small groups develop prayer, fellowship, study, recreation, or evangelism groups whose purpose is narrowly defined as the focus implies.

While there is nothing inherently wrong with this approach, it is necessary for the leader to clearly understand the small group's purpose and thus its nature. Frequently we fail because we structure groups to do things they were never designed to do and the leaders were never trained to carry out. Following are four primary purposes of a discipleship small group.

Leadership Development

Discipleship small groups exist to develop mature Christian leaders. Often students know well what they want, but little about what they need. The discipler will attempt to make the small group members aware of the opportunities and needs in the campus around them and their commissioning by Christ to that campus. They need to be challenged to develop vision (personally and corporately), and to have the character of Christ more firmly built within them. They need to experience leadership opportunities and the skills necessary to be a leader and to grow in leadership. They should be taught how to study the Bible and think for themselves and how to hear God's voice and obey Him.

Proper Pastoral Care and Spiritual Oversight

The small group experience provides students a place for spiritual and personal nurture. In this context, a trained discipler seeks to assist the newer believer in the development of their relationship with and understanding of Jesus. Help should come in making godly choices with regard to morals, resources, relationships, and vocation. The discipler will demonstrate, in a safe environment, an experience of spiritual leadership and submission to a caring authority.

Loving Relationships

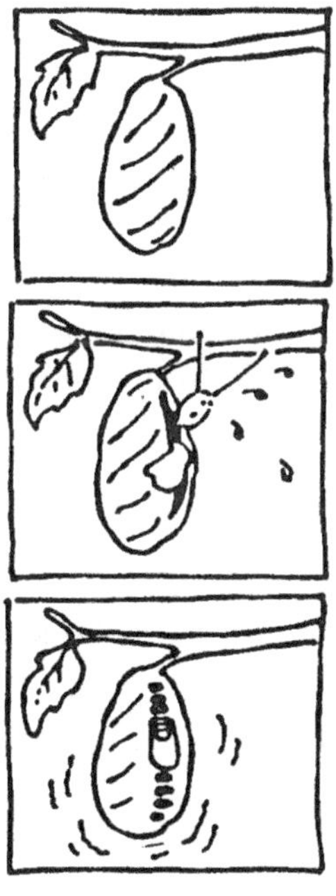

The small group is a place where confession of sin and forgiveness is expressed, where ministry to each other is facilitated by the work of the Holy Spirit through gifts of healing, faith, wisdom, etc. The small group is a place of mutual affirmation and vulnerability and, from this intimacy a sense of mutual accountability is fostered in this loving atmosphere. For many, the small group becomes a special family away from home.

Missional Life-style

The fourth purpose of a small group is exposing each student to God's purposes in His world. The one who loves God will demonstrate it by keeping His commandments. Students are challenged to put to death their deeply entrenched self-centeredness and be involved in reaching their campus and their world for Christ. Without this outward focus, the good inward focus will eventually begin to sour.

Essential Core Values for Discipleship Small Groups

Loving the Unlovable

A discipler must love each and every member of the group. Natural love will not suffice – she/he must be filled with the Spirit and express *agape* love. As a leader, you can do everything perfect in regard to structure, and reproduce ineffective disciples if you fail to love. On the other hand, a young leader could stumble and bumble along and yet still leave a lasting impact on his/her group's life because he/she loved them. Love does, in fact, cover a multitude of sins and ineptness.

Accepting the Unacceptable

Leaders are called on to express Kingdom values as opposed to cultural values. If a group is to be effective, a leader must accept people where they are and gently, with love, move them forward from there.

Forgiving the Unforgivable

We all fail. We fail to meet our own expectations as well as those of others. Most, if not all of us, have our battles of living under the law. If a disciple is to truly grow, he will do so best in an atmosphere of forgiveness and encouragement. In all things, apply a healthy does of grace. When sin occurs, lead the group through the biblical steps of confession, restitution, forgiveness, and reconciliation, ending with the affirmation of acceptance.

Confronting the Unconfronted

Sgt. O'Malley, implementing an experimental technique: Non–confrontive law enforcement.

We must love with a love based on truth and the other person's ultimate well-being in Christ in mind. Effective leaders will not be produced where there is not enough love to "speak the truth in love". But remember, speak it in love.

Lesson 8

Discipleship Through Small Groups II: Leadership Style & Community Building

Discipleship and Fellowship

I once heard Dr. Nicholas Tavani, a Christian Sociologist, say, "Fellowship only occurs in small groups." He means, fellowship (the purposeful and intimate sharing of our lives) cannot occur at a large group (over 12 people). He claims it is impossible for us to have significant, concurrent relationships with more than a dozen people. Surely the number of close friends through a lifetime would be much higher, but on any given day of our lives we can handle no more than a dozen. Most of us never come close to having a dozen close, concurrent friends. Probably most of our relationships are benevolent acquaintances. Some people never find a true close friend for major portions of their lives. However, Jesus modeled a lifestyle of personal openness and vulnerability. This is determinative for the way we relate to each other as Christians. Therefore, fellowship is a major aspect of a discipleship small group.

"What we have seen and heard we announce to you also, so that you will join us in the fellowship that we have with the Father and with his Son Jesus Christ. If we live in the light – just as he is in the light – then we have fellowship with one another, and the blood of Jesus, his Son, purifies us from every sin" (1 John 1:3, 7).

What Style of Leadership is Best Utilized in a Discipleship Small Group?

- "That guy acts like such a dictator!"
- "Why is he such a passive leader?"
- "I like our pastor because he is like a player/coach."

What makes a leader effective? Ted Engstrom cites a survey of 200 managers who overwhelmingly agreed the most important single skill of an executive is his ability to get along with people. "In the survey, management rated this ability more vital than intelligence, decisiveness, knowledge, or job skills." Ted Engstrom, *The Making of a Christian Leader 67*

A leadership style is the way a leader goes about his or her responsibilities and how the people perceive their leader. Experts in small group dynamics discovered a variety of group leadership styles. Some are more helpful than others, and some more appropriate at different stages in the small group's development.

Four common leadership styles include autocratic (domineering, command-and-control), authoritative (definite yet responsive), democratic (consensus building), and laissez-faire (permissive, passive).

The issue here is not, "Which leadership style is better than the others," but "Which style is best for this particular group at this stage of development?"

"Good evening. I am your new facilitator unit. I have the ability to access every verse of Scripture in every known dialect in less than..."

The most effective style shifts from an early position of control (or being directive) to a later position of facilitation (community and consensus-building). In the first 2 - 4 weeks, the small group members will be getting to know each other but be uncertain how to share with each other. A well prepared leader with a clear idea where he or she wants to go, who is open to discussion and the active involvement of the group members, must give the inexperienced group members a sense of direction and security that is helpful in the early stages of group life. The leader should model the kind of sharing he or she hopes will typify the entire year. This means the leader is the first to share (personal histories, testimonies, responses to discussion questions, etc.) and thus set an example for others to follow.

Following this first stage, the leader moves to a facilitator role. The members now begin to feel a sense of ownership of their group. They are aware of how to open up their lives to one another. Now the leader assists their sharing, highlights truths expressed, asks appropriate questions, and makes the necessary transitions in the meeting. Rather than being the first to share, he or she calls for dialogue or response from the members. The leader still is modeling transparency and affirmation, but in a less controlling manner. This is a shift from the authoritative to democratic style.

To restate, the best leadership practices emerge when prepared leaders offer suggestions and guidance most strongly in the beginning (authoritative) and move as rapidly as possible to a shared ownership of the group by all its members (democratic). By the end of the school year, the group members are exercising many of the functions in the group and sharing as equal partners in decision-making concerning their plans and procedures.

Stages in Group Life

Over the course of a school year, it is important for a small group leader to be aware of the stages of a small group. Small groups go through stages as they begin, continue, and end their life together. Just as an individual moves through stages in his lifecycle from infancy to old age, so groups move through stages as well. There are at least four stages a discipleship small group will go through to achieve effectiveness.

A. History Giving

"You too? I thought I was the only one who tortured small rodents before eating them."

In healthy relationships, the prerequisite to love is knowing. For a discipleship small group to go from a collection of people to a community of love, an atmosphere of love and acceptance needs to be facilitated. This is best accomplished by allowing people to share their backgrounds, their personal histories. Tell stories from their past that contribute to their present identity? Hopes and dreams need to be expressed as well as life goals, successes, and failures.

So share your personal stories from your past. Start with sharing stories that are the least threatening and even fun to disclose. If your group plans to stay together from 12 to 30 weeks, then spend the first 2 to 4 weeks with a focus on history giving. Lay a foundation of mutual understanding. It is important to process relationship before task.

B. Affirmation

You feel affirmed when you share something personal and a core of people show genuine interest and care. So make affirmation the primary purpose of a small group meeting. It's an opportunity to verbalize your growing love and concern for each other.

Share with each other the strengths and Christian character qualities you are observing in your small group members. Warmly express your acceptance of your new friends. Immediately after you've completed the history-giving stage, schedule one meeting to affirm one another. Periodically (once every 8-10 weeks) schedule an affirmation session again. Learn to demonstrate your love in actions and in words.

A further note on History-Giving and Affirmation:

One natural history-giving exercise is for everyone to tell their testimony of receiving Christ. The leader should share first. Take your time. It will give you a good hint as where people are on their spiritual journey. This will also assist each person in gaining the same self-understanding.

A good book for these first two phases of group life is the *Serendipity Bible for Groups*. It combines an NIV Bible with relational questions to aid in group sharing and discussion of each passage of the Bible.

C. Discipleship

Discipleship need not and should not be a static educational experience. It is best accomplished in a vibrant relational context. It is a shame to take the Words of Life and express them in lifeless forms. So into this loving atmosphere of mutual accountability, begin to live out the process of discipleship exemplified by Jesus.

Individual needs should be assessed and biblical goals are highlighted. There are skills to be learned (Bible study, prayer, witnessing, etc.), there are healings (physical, emotional, relational), and there are truths that must be comprehended and integrated. All this best occurs when friends accept us, and give us the support and practical help necessary for us to accomplish our spiritual development goals. In a year of small group life, discipleship will be the dominant focus.

D. Close Fellowship

This last phase is more a statement of realized purpose than an actual phase of small group life. Close fellowship reminds us the discipleship small group is not an end in itself – it is the communion of hearts and minds. The ultimate purpose is to fulfill the great commandments as Jesus expressed them – to love God with our whole being and love our neighbor as ones self.

The small group is an excellent structure where communion may occur. However, close fellowship is not guaranteed because one joins a small group. If people are to grow in love for God and others, they must obey the commands of Christ. Communion of souls and minds is hard to plan for. It is most often found spontaneously erupting when God's people gather in His name to fulfill His desires.

A Potpourri of Questions Regarding Small Group Life

How large should a small group become?

Experience demonstrates 4 to 6 people to be the ideal size. Remember, the larger the group, the less personal "air-time" and thus the slower the relational growth. Groups larger than 6 need co-leaders and significant contact with one another outside the small group meeting.

How long should a small group meeting last?

I think 2 hours is necessary to accomplish the purposes and goals of a small group meeting.

How often should the small group meetings occur and when?

The pace of the university scene is fast and changing. Much happens from one day to the next. So stay current with each other. It seems best to have a meeting once every week. The best times are in the evenings, but many successful groups have also met in the late afternoon or Saturday mornings.

Should discipleship small groups be coed or sexually segregated?

While both have merit, the most successful groups are the sexually segregated (men's and women's) groups. Issues of self-image, problems stemming from the past, plus personal intimate issues are of great concern to college students. Coed groups may be too inhibiting and they require great maturity. The segregated groups seem to enhance commitment and reduce game-playing between people.

Just a note of observation for what it's worth: I have noticed the majority of students truly prefer segregated groups. Often the requests for coed groups come from men and the strongest supporters of segregated groups are the women. As a general rule it is much more difficult for men to be open and communicative with other men, yet it is a essential area for personal growth among college males.

The Essential Ingredient: Commitment

It doesn't take a great person to be a believer; but it does, however, require all there is of him. If doing things that feel good is the controlling motivation of a person, then he will not become a dependable people. Commitment opens the door to growth. Commitments force us to make choices, and our choices highlight our priorities. Our choices have consequences both positive and negative.

I think the lack of commitment is like a slipping clutch on a car. The driver has years of experience, the car is well tuned and powerful, the road is smooth, but the clutch will not engage. It can be the same with in a small group. The leader can be well trained and the members can have good, warm Christian hearts, but without commitment, the small group will flounder. Commitment is an essential ingredient to the development of a trust-filled core. Commitment must be taught, expected, and modeled.

Make the issue of commitment the very first item of discussion at the very first small group meeting. Use a covenant sheet as a tool for discussion. (See the Appendix) A group covenant will define the expectations and limits of the commitment. Don't fudge on this issue. If someone cannot declare their willingness to comply with the minimum commitments, then suggest that they wait until their schedule or priorities shift so they can subscribe to the group commitments.

Lesson 9

Discipleship Through Small Groups III: Format, Formation & Content

In this lesson, I continue to examine the dynamics of developing a discipleship small group. The previous two lessons discussed the purposes and phases for these groups. In this lesson, the discussion moves to the format, formation and content of these small group meetings. But before we do, let's look briefly at an important issue concerning discipline and deliverance in discipleship.

Discipleship Involves Both Discipline and Deliverance

The ultimate purpose of a Christian is to know God the Father in a personal and intimate way, to become like Jesus His Son, and, by the power of the Holy Spirit, to live like Jesus. However, we all have been born into sin and have gratified "the cravings of our sinful nature and (followed) its desires and thoughts. Like the rest, we were by nature objects of wrath." (Ephesians 2:3) This indicates we've been thwarted in our ultimate purpose.

We are in desperate need of an inner transformation. This Jesus offers to us full and free through faith by virtue of His triumph on the cross and the grave. We stand forgiven before the Father and fully adopted into His family.

Nonetheless, we discover on-going growth in Christ is still needed in us all. We still must put our past to death in Christ, and clothe ourselves with the newness Jesus offers.

For Jesus to bring freedom into our lives, we need both deliverance and discipline. Deliverance is an encounter with Christ by the Spirit. He may deal with evil forces harassing our lives, freedom from habitual sin, or healing for our body, mind or soul. These are moments Jesus comes strongly into our life and breaks the power enslaving us. From that moment, we experience freedom such as we have never known before. God intervened and we are different from that time on.

Discipline, on the other hand, is not instantaneous. It is by nature experienced over time. Discipline is repentance lived out. When we repent of our sin, we must turn from it for repentance to be real and complete. The spiritual disciplines are ways we continue to express repentance and turn our life over to the Lord. When we discard discipline for the guise of freedom, we are in essence rationalizing away our repentance. Thus, it is the delivered and disciplined man that grows up into the fullness of Christ.

The gospel writers tell us the story of the feeding of the 5,000. Jesus instructed the disciples to divide the crowd into smaller groups of 50 each. Anyone who has ever worked with large groups of people might see in the successful accomplishment of this task a miracle. But the miracle was not in the creation of order. The miracle occurred with the intervention of God in multiplying the food.

Order and freedom go hand in hand. The disciplines build order in our lives. The creation of order where there has been chaos brings health to us. But it also prepares our lives for God's Spirit to bring even greater freedom to us.

We need both order and freedom in our lives. The discipling process emphasizes both regular discipline that promotes orderliness, and occasional deliverance that brings freedom.

Discipleship in a small group is the foremost biblical context for deliverance and discipline to be fostered. Deliverance is most often experienced in a body ministry context. Discipline is best fostered where mutually supportive relationships exist. Discipleship is Jesus' idea for spiritual growth.

The Small Group Meeting Format

How should a typical small group meeting flow? How do you start and end, and what do you do in the middle? What are the core components of a small group meeting that promote sharing, learning and growing in Christ?

A. Worship

In a discipleship small group, worship could be anything from conversational prayer and a song, to 45 minutes of total focus of adoration of God through song, scripture, and spiritual gifts. No doubt the comfort level of the individual members will determine your worship experience. Whatever expression it takes, worship is a time to transition from the concerns of the day to coming together with other believers to praise God from whom all wisdom and strength comes.

B. Content

"What did Isaiah mean by that? How 'bout you, Doug? We haven't heard much from you tonight."

From worship we move to the study phase. This is the appropriate time to teach skills such as Bible study, prayer, and witnessing. Or the focus could go to an inductive Bible study through a New Testament book. The choice of subject matter is almost endless. Whatever material is covered, some principles in this interaction time are important to remember:

- The content phase should have a primary goal of calling each member to a personal application to carry out during the next few days or weeks.
- The teaching should be done in a discussion mode and not after a lecture style.
- Learning should be accomplished by assisted self-discovery. The members should be encouraged to be mutually supportive

of each other's applications. Everyone needs to be involved, learning, and sharing.

C. Sharing

The handicap of a content-only-oriented-meeting is it often misses the personal needs the members bring with them to the small group meeting. The small group is a place to stay current with each other. To update one another of the joys and sorrows of the past week, to express praise to the Lord for the answers to prayer, or to tell one another the needs each person is facing. Without this sharing time, the small group will grow relationally stale.

D. Prayer

Now that you have heard each member's application to the Bible study and/or their need expressed in the sharing time, you can pray very specifically for each other. Close fellowship grows between people when they pray for each other. When the answers to prayer start to return to the group, zeal for God breaks out! Through prayer for each other, the members will recognize God truly does care and love them dearly.

"Chuck, let's start with you. What would you say was the most significant thing that's happened to you lately?"

This format is to be used as a tool and not as a club. Going from one phase to the next should facilitate growth and encouragement to all the members. But don't hold to this format rigidly. If worship is flowing especially well one night, let it happen. If someone comes into the meeting obviously distressed, minister to him immediately rather than waiting until the sharing phase to recognize your friend's need. And if one phase seems to stall one night, then suggest a move to the next phase. A small group leader will find this to be a very helpful framework within which to operate.

Some additional tips on how to lead worship, discussion, sharing and prayer in a small group.

A. Worship

- Divide the group in half and read responsively a passage you have chosen. The Psalms are great for this.
- Ask someone before the meeting to prepare a testimony of God working in her life over the past week.
- Sing songs familiar to everyone, songs everyone knows all the words to. If you are going to teach a new song, take time to do so and then sing it through several times.
- If you lack musical talent, play a few songs from a DVD and encourage everyone to sing along.
- Encourage anyone with musical talent to bring an instrument and keep on encouraging him to grow in leading worship with you.
- Type out the words to songs and sing off song sheets.
- Have a talented member come prepared to share some music to begin the night.
- Open a group time with a response to God in silence, giving a verse or thought to meditate on.
- As you sing, have them change their posture (bowing, kneeling, standing, lifting hands, lying prostrate).
- Give them a theme (like God's faithfulness, God's love) and have them pray one-sentence prayers around this theme.

B. Discussion during Content phase

- Remember, in the early stages of your group, you need to ask the questions and be the first one to respond. Model the manner you hope they will share.
- Ask questions that cannot be answered with "yes" or "no". For instance:
    - What do you see in this passage…
    - What is your response to…
    - How do you feel about…
    - If the apostle Paul wrote this to you, what would you…
    - What in your life corresponds to verse…

- When someone asks you a question, bounce it back at the group. "That's a great question, Josh. Matt, how would you answer it?"
- Direct questions at normally quiet people to draw them out, and then affirm them immediately after they've talked.
- When the group gets off on an unproductive tangent, say so and encourage them to go back to the original issue by restating the issue.

C. Sharing

- Focus on becoming current with each other. Ask questions that get at that kind of information. For example:
    - What has God been saying to you during the past week?
    - What was the greatest thing that you experienced this past week?
    - What was the most difficult thing you faced lately?
- Ask them to report-in concerning the things you previously prayed about.
- Share your feelings first if you sense the group is a little hesitant that night. What is the primary agenda going on in your life and how you feel about it?
- Tell them to listen very closely to what the person on their left shares, because you are going to ask they pray for that person later.
- At times you may need to be very direct by asking someone who is unusually quiet how things are going.
- Before, during, and after meetings, affirm your members, showing your appreciation for their openness. Don't do this every night, but often enough to prove your sincerity.

D. Prayer

"...and please, God, let me find a large bloated mammal by the side of the road on my way home tonight..." "Say, whose prayer request is this, anyway?"

- Pray for people's application to the Bible study or the concern they mentioned during the sharing time.
- Put one member in the middle of the circle and have everyone gather around and pray for them. Then move to the next member and do the same.
- Encourage students to pray for the person on their right/left and pray out loud so all may agree together.
- Suggest everyone close with sentence prayers and pray as often as they would like.
- Pick a country or a need on campus and make that the prayer focus.
- Get into a football huddle or have everyone hold hands as they pray.
- Spend an entire night in prayer. Go through the ACTS format phase by phase. (See lesson 10)
- Focus on one thing such as "thanksgiving" or "God's love."
- Take 10 minutes to write out a prayer, and then read it to everyone.

How to form a Discipleship Small Group

Briefly, remember what you're hoping to create: a context where students gather together weekly for mutual love, training, encouragement, accountability, and growth in the Lord. At the beginning they may not know each other, but they need to make commitments to each other if true spiritual growth is going to occur. Frankly, that this would ever happen is a real miracle! This is exactly what you trust Jesus to do – use you to create a miracle! How does this miracle come into being?

A. *Pray* earnestly for God to lead you to the faithful men or women He desires you to pour you life into. Pray the students He leads you to are freshmen and sophomores, along with praying for the upperclassmen the Lord has already placed in your life by friendship.

B. *Make Contact* with as many new people as possible. Move into your dorm room early and assist others as they move in. Man a booktable in your dorm lobby. Put an invitation to a small group Bible study on your door. Wear a campus ministry T-shirt. Check with the campus ministry staff for leads on new students. Introduce yourself to visitors at the main weekly meeting or visitors at your local church. Be creative! Do whatever you can to meet as many people as possible in the first 4 weeks of each school term. Do so with a genuine attitude of concern for your new friends. Check your heart motivation throughout this process.

C. *Explain* what a discipleship small group is to the new friends you are making. Describe the impact it had on your life and why you feel it is important. These opportunities may provide a chance for you to share your testimony to someone who has never heard it clearly.

D. *Invite* the person to come at a time and place you have predetermined. Explain the level of commitment necessary for a good small group (maybe even leave with them a copy of a commitment sheet for them to look at and bring to the meeting). When they say they would like to attend you will need to remind them often of the time and place (probably you will need to go by and pick them up for the first small group meeting). If they are interested, but can't come at that time, you should introduce them to a small group leader whose group meets at a time more convenient. Invite and walk with them to a main weekly meeting.

E. *Plan* carefully for the first 4 meetings. Make sure everyone understands the issues surrounding commitment, and then invest time in history giving and prayer for each other. Be organized. Have most of the details planned before the start of the semester so that you can devote most of your time to making friends and follow-up. The top priority is building friendship among all the members.

F. *Pray* some more. Trust God to perform a miracle before your eyes by providing contacts, interest, conviction, friendship and commitment. These things coming together are always a miracle of God's Spirit working hand-in-hand with our efforts.

The Content of a Discipleship Small Group

Now you have a group of students becoming friends with each other, what do you disciple them in? What do you attempt to teach them? Below is a list of potential subjects to consider. You will not be able to cover all of these in one school year by any means, but they may help you identify where your group needs to go next.

1. Bible Study Skills
2. Scripture Memory
3. Personal Prayer Life
4. Worship
5. Personal Evangelism
6. Relationship Building Skills
7. Lordship of Christ
8. Essential Christian Beliefs
9. Spiritual Disciplines
10. Faithfulness & Commitment
11. Management of Time & Money
12. Spiritual Gifts
13. Leadership Practices & Skills
14. Christian sexuality
15. Self-esteem
16. God's Will & Guidance
17. Assurance of Salvation
18. Christian Missions
19. Life in the Spirit
20. Dealing with Temptation, Sin, Satan

Beyond these topics probably the best decision is to study of a book of the Bible. Every biblical book has a central theme. Choose a book that addresses the consensus needs of the group members. For example, you might choose:

- Psalms - to discover worship
- Amos - to learn about social justice
- The Gospel of Mark - to deal with servanthood
- The Gospel of Luke - to study the work of the Spirit in Jesus
- Galatians - to distinguish between living under law or grace
- Ephesians - to learn about the body of Christ
- 1 Thessalonians - to teach on discipleship

- James - to focus on practical Christianity
- 1 Peter - to study suffering as a Christian

How do you go about choosing the content for your Small Group?

A. Evaluate your group

Look at a list like the ones above and then evaluate your group. What areas of weaknesses or interests are in your group members?

Looking at his small group, Earl began to see a common point of weakness.

B. Recognize need

Assist your members in understanding and recognizing this area of growth. Help them to own the issue or growth area.

C. Address Need by Scripture

Go to the Word of God for solutions, directions, and instruction. Early in the school year you need to teach them a simple Bible study method because you can then build upon this foundation all year long and, enable them to feed themselves from the Word when you're not around.

D. Establish goals

Highlight very carefully the goals you are working toward. They need to know what you are trying to achieve together.

E. Follow-up with pastoral care

Pray with each person as they try to implement the new skill or grow in their Christian walk.

Lesson 10

One-to-One Discipleship From the Small Group Context

In Lesson 7 I suggested the ideal model for discipleship is a small group supported by one-to-one coaching. Lessons 7-9 focused on the biblical example and practical skills of small group discipleship. Secondary to it, but also essential, is time spent one-to-one between the discipling leader and the new disciple.

One-to-One discipleship raises a new set of questions: What occurs during these meetings? What do we talk about? How can this time be invested in a quality manner? Answering these questions and teaching the skills of one-to-one discipleship are the goals of this lesson.

A Strategy for 1-to-1 Discipleship

Build a trust-filled relationship

"Boy this is embarassing. Here's the first photo of me. That's my sister Clara on the left."

Keep in mind discipleship flows from a relational context. Nowhere is this more obvious than sitting in the student union face-to-face with a new disciple. The guiding principle is, "Process relationship before task." It is necessary in the initial times together for the new disciple to be assured she/he is more important for who they are than for what they do or believe. Before you teach them skills, be very careful to underscore the importance of your mutual relationship. Be personal rather than "religious". Let them know who you are, and how Christ is transforming your life. Let them see they are not the only person on the planet with problems and doubts and that Christians are real people, too.

Therefore, do more in-depth personal history sharing. Learn as much as you can about the person, while at the same time letting him know you more fully. Since one of the strengths of one-to-one is it fosters discussions at a deeper level, then work to build on this strength. Since love is built on knowing, this then requires openness on your part. In this way you are expressing trust in the person and showing that you care. Do all you can (from your side) to build a trust-filled relationship.

Teach them how to study the Bible

One of the most important skills you pass on to a new believer is the ability to study the Word of God. Study goes beyond devotional reading. You goal is to help a disciple with the same challenge Paul gave to Timothy, "Do your best to present yourself to God as one approved, a workman who does not need to be ashamed and who correctly handles the word of truth." 2 Timothy 2:15

What follows provides the nuts-and-bolts for method of biblical interpretation. I offer you the core procedure for bible study and with it a bible study tool you may use in the one-to-one context.

There are three components of a good Bible study methodology. The primary goal for the study of Scripture is to arrive at the meaning of the passage. This meaning needs to be discovered in three stages:

- First, Observation: This always occurs first. One seeks to discover the facts and structure of the passage in order to lay a foundation for interpretation.
- Second, Interpretation: Here we intend to answer the question, "What did this passage mean to the first readers?" What was the author's purpose of writing?
- Third, Application: This is where the meaning of the passage to the first readers is translated into our present day

situation. It answers the question, "What does this passage mean to me?"

Our first aim in biblical interpretation is to determine the meaning the author intended to communicate to his audience. Therefore, the meaning of a passage must be something the original readers could have understood. Stated differently, a biblical text cannot mean today what it could not have meant when it was written. Only after we have a good idea of what the text meant there-and-then can we go on to see what the text means for us here-and-now.

Here is a Bible study tool you can use. PROAPT is an acrostic for: Pray, Read, Observe, Apply, Pray, and Tell. See appendix 8 and 9.

Pray

Quiet yourself before going to God's Word. This can be a short time of prayer or lengthy. Be sure to include as a part of the prayer time: "Dear Lord, please speak to me from your Word and by your Spirit today."

Read

Read the passage aloud. If possible, read the passage in different translations. Make every effort to involve as many of the physical senses, as possible.

Observe

Now is the time to write down all that you observe from the text. In your observation, answer some of the following questions:

- Who are the people mentioned, where (location) does this passage happen, when did it occur?
- What literary constructions are significant, i.e., repetitions, comparisons and contrasts, verb tenses, cause and effect?
- What kind of literature (genre) is this, i.e., history, teaching material, poetry, prophecy, parable?
- What do the words mean? Look up important words in a dictionary and substitute the definition for the word and reread the passage.

- Is there any progression or logical development of thought in this passage?
- What is the main point of this passage?
- What did the first readers understand the first time they read this text?

I suggest you try to outline or paraphrase the passage trying to rephrase the meaning by using your own words.

Apply

Now it is time to bridge the gap between the there-and-then and the here-and-now by asking these questions:

- What issue does this passage raise that are still issues today?
- What does this passage say about my relationship with God and with other people, about sin in my life and about my attitudes?
- What truth may I apply within the next 48 hours?
- What behavior does this passage call for that I am not now doing?

Application is the most difficult part of any Bible study method to master. We tend to make applications that are generalized wishes. We often come away from the biblical text with goals too large or non-specific. So chop up the gigantic applications into bite-size chunks. The key for great application of Scripture is to be specific!

Take the following example: "Lord I want to be more disciplined in my Bible study." While admirable there is no objective criteria with which progress can be measured. Break it down like this: "Lord, in an effort to become more disciplined in my personal Bible study, I am committing to spend from 7:30 to 8:00 AM on Mondays, Wednesdays, and Fridays doing my PROAPTs through Philippians." This makes the application specific according to purpose (Bible study), time (7:30-8:00 MWF), and method (PROAPT).

Pray

Again, at this point, commit to Jesus your application and praise Him for speaking to you.

Tell

Find a prayer partner, preferably someone in your small group. Let them know what Jesus is saying and doing in you. These reports may become some of the most quality conversations in your life.

One final recommendation: when PROAPTing, build depth and consistency in your study by parking on the same biblical book or on the same biblical topic. It is better to invest deeply in one place at a time. A lifetime of consistent focused study will reap a bounty of fruit.

In your one-to-one sessions follow this suggested strategy: Demonstrate how to use the PROAPT method for bible study. Ask the new disciple to do three PROAPTs per week for the next two weeks. Two weeks later meet with them and go over their PROAPTs with him/her. Discover together areas where improvement could be made. Repeat this assignment until the new disciple comes to a level of mastery of this bible study tool.

The PROAPT model is adapted from Discipling Ministries Seminar, Barnabas, Inc. Used by permission, 1991.

Teach them how to pray

Alongside the ability to study the bible, another essential skill is learning how to pray. Since the disciples asked Jesus how to pray, it is certainly appropriate for us to ask and learn! When you examine the Lord's Prayer, you will discover a few components in prayer. A tool reflecting these components is the **ACTS** format of prayer. **ACTS** is an acrostic for:

- Adoration: Praise to God for who He is (focus upon His character and nature).
- Confession: Declaring Jesus as Lord of your life and asking for the forgiveness of sin.
- Thanksgiving: Praise to God for what He has done (focus on His deeds).
- Supplication: Interceding for your needs and the needs of others.

Learning how to pray after this manner is a stretching experience for any disciple. Again, request in your one-to-one session they pray following this format three times per week for two weeks. Then after the sixth time, ask them to write out their reflections and thoughts. This will lead to a good discussion on prayer. Don't presume they will pray this way forever. But it is a great way to open them up to a deeper prayer life. Make prayer an anchor in the new disciple's life by spending time together praying in your one-to-ones. The ACTS format coupled with praying together will help a disciple learn to communicate with God.

Carefully assess personal needs

Ministering to another person begins with knowing their needs. By getting in touch with the stressors in their life it will assist you in knowing how to encourage them in spiritual growth. What is your purpose here? You are affirming confidence in a God who is able to meet us where we live. You are affirming your faith in God as you set an agenda for what you believe the Lord can do.

After you anchor in the spiritual disciplines of bible study and prayer, take an hour with this sheet in hand and ask them to describe their life in the four areas identified on the sheet: *personal & relational, family, academic*, and *spiritual*. This helps the person to gain an overview of the stressors in their life. From this perspective, you can then move toward addressing some specific areas of needed growth in the disciple.

Help them to set personal spiritual growth goals

"I've had this vision of myself one day having these big beautiful wings...and then migrating for thousands of miles...what'ya think? Is that crazy?"

The *ABC's of Ministry* is a strategy action sheet. It suggests a plan of action for the discipler and new believer to scale the mountains in his life. Again, it provides a framework for a healthy thinking process. It addresses the issues of purpose statements (what God designs for us). It also develops goals (how to walk in faith toward God's designs).

It is beneficial to use the sheet with the disciple. It visually helps her to see the process at hand. It pushes the discipler and new believer beyond vague wishes and to take meaningful steps of faith.

This sheet is not only for needs. When you deal with the first step, *Assess the Need*, you may select a talent or gift. For example: a desire to learn how to lead worship, or witness to a roommate, or stand up for Christ in class.

Remember, it is absolutely essential to do all the steps, especially step six – *Establish Proper Support*. Not only will you find this process useful in one-to-ones, but *The ABC's of Ministry* highlight the basic process of ministry in many contexts. Think in terms of the needs of your whole small group or even in terms of your entire campus ministry. The *ABCs* illustrate a process for ministry whether you are dealing with one person or one hundred.

The ABC's of Ministry. I'll examine each stage, one point at a time.

First, Assess the Need: After using the *Needs, Concerns and Stressors* sheet, then select one area of concern. Usually it is best the first time, to allow the new disciple to pick the area they want to grow in. If they select it, they will probably bring motivation to the task, thus increasing the likelihood for growth. Even if you believe another area is needed more, it is still better for them to choose the first area. They will be more willing to tackle other issues after they grow more comfortable with the process. Write out as clearly as possible the issue of need in the space provided, just so everyone has a clear understanding on the issue.

Second, Build a Biblical Foundation: What does God's Word have to say about this issue? Often the bible is direct and to the point. There are other times when finding the counsel in God's Word is more difficult. Here you are modeling the use of the Bible as the guide for all faith and practice. Carefully help the disciple see how we live under the authority of God's truth rather than by any standards imposed by contemporary morality. In this space, write a summary statement of the counsel from the bible with several scripture references listed.

Third, Create Measurable Goals: From the counsel of scripture, what should the disciple trust the Lord to do in his or her life? It is important for goals be specific and measurable. Vague goals are frustrating and you are never sure if you are making any progress. State the goals in terms of how much, when, how often, with whom, and where. Make the goals tangible and faith-filled. What is a good goal? "A goal is a statement about how we hope things are going to be at some time in the future. It is a statement of faith. Notice that goals are not statements about what will be. That is in God's hands. But they are statements about what we believe God wants us to do or to be, in light of his word."

Fourth, Develop a Plan of Action: Take your goals and write a strategic statement. Break it down into stages or steps. What will the disciple do first, then next, and then after that? If the goal will take three months to accomplish, what will the disciple do in the first month, the second and the third? Be specific and clear.

Lastly, Establish Proper Support: We were never intended to walk out our faith in Jesus alone. Christ has placed us carefully in his body. Therefore, we need to be there for each other. Establish times for evaluation and tweaking. Encouragement is always needed. Sometimes you will need to challenge the disciple stay on target. Sometimes she/he may need your forgiveness when they fail. Express compassion immediately. Check up regularly and commit yourself to see this process through with the disciple.

Ministry Skills Should Be Transgenerational

I believe discipleship is a transgenerational process whereby the message and methods of Jesus impact the world. The *skills or tools* used in this lesson need to be transgenerational, as well. *A transgenerational skill is when you teach one disciple by using skills they in turn can use to teach another later.*

This is why the forms used in this lesson are simple. There is nothing special or sacred in the forms. This is deliberate. The forms could be easily reproduced on a napkin at your favorite restaurant. They merely describe a process in ministry.

Remember the adage: don't just give a hungry man a fish, but teach him how to fish and thereby feed him for a lifetime. Don't just tell someone to go from A to Z, but show them how to go from A to Z. In doing so they will some day take someone else from A to Z. Keep the first skills you use simple and transgenerational. No doubt later on you will become much more sophisticated, but make sure the new disciple has something in their hand they can pass on to another.

Lesson 11

Forgiveness and Restoration

I include this lesson because personal and corporate discipline is crucial to the discipling process. It's a topic receiving little attention and even less application. More than that, some attempts at discipline are either so harsh or so anemic many people have soured on the topic.

What are we to do when a brother is slipping off the path or has fallen altogether? Forgiveness and restoration is central to the discipling process. How do failure, forgiveness, and restoration work together? How do we walk the delicate line between being tender and tough? Let's examine this sensitive issue.

Discipleship and Discipline

"My brothers, if one of you wanders away from the truth and another brings him back again, remember this: whoever turns a sinner back from his wrong way will save that sinner's soul and bring forgiveness of many sins." James 5:19, 20 TEV

Suddenly Carl is spotted. The relief his friends feel would be complete, if not for their guilt at letting him wander this far from home.

Disciples wander away from the truth for many reasons. Jesus warns some will have truth snatched from them by Satan. Others never go beyond the initial joy of salvation. Still others fall away due to trouble, persecution, or through the deceitfulness of wealth and desires for other things. See Mark 4:1-20

For some, they really don't lose their faith as much as they just cease to use their faith. This neglect results in coldness in their relationship with Christ, and they begin to renege on their commitment. Double-mindedness sets in. The Book of James reminds us, "he who doubts is like a wave of the sea, blown and tossed by the wind. That man should not think he will receive anything from the Lord; he is a double-minded man, unstable in all he does." James 1:6b-8

There is little written on bringing restoration to a person in a local body when he goes astray or is jammed up in sin. No doubt this topic makes many nervous due to gross mistakes they have heard about or witnessed firsthand. There is a tendency to avoid the issue altogether. Pervasive individualism in our society is prevalent in our fellowship groups and churches, thereby causing many to consider intervention into someone's life an intrusion or an infringement upon one's personal privacy. We come to believe it is inappropriate to ever question someone else, fearing we have overstepped our bounds or that we are being judgmental.

But when one considers the instructions given to us in the Scriptures concerning the interdependency of believers one to another, we should not be surprised to see instructions such as Matthew 18:15-20 and Galatians 6:1-5.

"If your brother sins against you, go to him and show him his fault. But do it privately, just between yourselves.... If he listens to you, you have won your brother back. But if he will not listen to you, take one or two other persons with you, so that 'every accusation may be upheld by the testimony of two or more witnesses,' as the scripture says. And if he will not listen to them, then tell the whole thing to the church. Finally, if he will not listen to the church, treat him as though he were a pagan or a tax collector." Matthew 18:15-17 TEV

"My brothers, if someone is caught in any kind of wrongdoing, those of you who are spiritual should set him right; but you must do it in a gentle way. And keep an eye on yourselves, so that you will not be tempted, too. Carry each other's burdens, and in this way you will fulfill the law of Christ. If anyone thinks he is something when he is nothing, he deceives himself. Each one should judge his own conduct. If it is good, then he can be proud of what he himself has done, without having to compare it with what someone else has done. For everyone has to carry his own load." Galatians 6:1-5

These passages call for direct and definite initiation toward someone in the body who is struggling in their Christian walk. This then is a vital issue for all who intend to be disciplers. It is an essential responsibility in the process of discipleship.

Discipline For the Wayward Disciple

Let's recall some things mentioned from a previous lesson. "Discipline is training that amends, molds, and sharpens the mental abilities and moral character of a person. Often our first thought is of punishment when we consider discipline, but even good correction should serve to put right a person due to their lack of self-control (trusting that this direct attention will aid in the development of self-control). Thus, to discipline simply means to impose order upon disorder within the mind, heart and spirit."

Every disciple submits to Godly discipline. The writer of Hebrews tells us "God disciplines us for our good, that we may share in his holiness."

"Endure hardship as discipline; God is treating you as sons. For what son is not disciplined by his father? If you are not disciplined (and everyone undergoes discipline), then you are illegitimate children and not true sons. Moreover, we have all had human fathers who disciplined us and we respected them for it. How much more should we submit to the Father of our spirits and live! Our fathers disciplined us for a little while as they thought best; but God disciplines us for our good, that we may share in his holiness. No discipline seems pleasant at the time, but painful. Later on, how ever, it produces a harvest of righteousness and peace for those who have been trained by it." Hebrews 12:7-11

Lesson six focused on the spiritual disciplines and self-discipline. This lesson focuses on exercise of discipline necessary to bring back a brother or sister who is wandering from the truth. Their eternal life is at stake.

In Lesson 8 I pointed out "discipline is repentance lived out." To discipline a brother caught in sin, is to bring them back to the foundations of their salvation and their relationship with God. It means to speak the message of grace again to them and to call upon them to repent from their folly. How are we to carry out this process of discipline?

The Occasion for Discipline: "If Your Brother Sins"

"If your brother sins against you, go and show him his fault...." Mt. 18:15a Scholars debate the meaning of "against you" in this passage. Some feel it refers only to sin that injures you directly. Others feel "against you" suggests you are a witness to the problem. Probably both positions have merit. In fact, many of the ancient manuscripts omitted the words "against you" in this passage. This would make the injunction even simpler. If you are aware your brother is in sin, then you are to go to him.

Neglect is not excusable. Too often we sound like Cain when he said to God, "Am I my brother's keeper?" This passage seems to underscore, since we are brothers and sisters in Christ, we have a responsibility to one another. One of these responsibilities is to care enough for each other to intervene during times of spiritual waywardness.

The spiritual life is a reality where sin and righteousness are mutually exclusive. Consequently, even if acts of sin are concealed, the symptoms of spiritual illness will eventually surface somewhere. When the revealing signs of sin make their appearance, a discipler is obliged to inquire into the life of the individual in question. This is not a matter of prying into the private life of people; it is an attempt to help them return to the way of faith. Thus, a fellowship group does not go around looking for hidden sins. As in evangelism, so in discipline, we are looking for discipleship, which by its nature is open and visible.

What specific sins should concern us? In Galatians 5 Paul mentions in three consecutive paragraphs, first the "deeds of the flesh," second, the "fruits of the Spirit," and finally he gives instructions on how to restore a brother caught in sin. As you pan back even further in this chapter Paul is talking about finding "freedom in Christ." For Paul restoring a brother caught in sin is an issue of restoring a person back to a place of freedom. It is clear to see the specific sins on Paul's heart and mind. Here is a brief description of the "deeds of the flesh."

DEEDS OF THE FLESH FROM GALATIANS 5:19-21	
Immorality	...is primarily referring to sexual immorality of any kind. It was so common in Greco-Roman antiquity it was not regarded as especially reprehensible. Our culture is not much different.
Impurity	...is like an unclean wound or an unpruned tree. To be impure means one can't approach a holy God.
Sensuality	...is a readiness for any pleasure with no restraint for any desire. Hedonism as a doctrine proclaims pleasure and happiness as the sole or chief end in life.
Idolatry	...is where material things take the place of God. Our Western culture doesn't promote the erection of statues for worship, but it does promote the worship of power, fame, wealth, security, etc. Idolatry is any substitute for the living and true God.

DEEDS OF THE FLESH FROM GALATIANS 5:19-21	
Sorcery	...is literally "the use of drugs", primarily for use in witchcraft. Drug use and the rise of the occult are issues our culture struggles to deal with effectively.
Hatred	...is hostile sentiments, intentions, or acts. Examples are numerous (child abuse, wife abuse, rape, terrorism, international aggression) and each one is being experienced today in excessive proportions
Strife	...is rivalry resulting in quarrels and power struggles. The opposite of strife is peace.
Jealousy	...is the desire to have what someone else has. Jealousy breeds resentment, bitterness, suspicion, insecurity and anxiety - a real green-eyed monster.
Outbursts of Anger	...are bursts of temper, anger that strikes out physically, verbally, or emotionally.
Selfish Ambition	...describes the man who wants office, not from any altruistic motives of service, but for what he can get out of it. Pure self-interest.
Dissension	...is where members of a group fly apart instead of come together. It is a disagreement leading to discord and disunity.
Factions	...are cliques of people who hold different views and end up disliking not each other's views, but each other.
Envy	...begrudges the fact someone has things at all. The grudging spirit cannot bear to contemplate someone else's prosperity or good fortune.

DEEDS OF THE FLESH FROM GALATIANS 5:19-21	
Drunkenness	...is excessive indulgence in strong drink weakening the rational and moral control over words and actions. Unilaterally hailed by administrators and students as the number one problem on campus.
Carousing	...is normally associated with drunkenness. It is probably equivalent to what the university community calls "partying." It is unrestrained revelry, enjoyment that degenerates into license.

A common thread woven through this list is each is a sin against a relationship in some form. This list is not intended to be conclusive. But a discipler is addressing an important issue when dealing with something off this list.

The Goal of Discipline: "If He Repents Then Forgive"

Remember, the essential goal of discipline is not to correctly follow the specific instructions in restoration but to win our brother back through repentance to God. Let me draw a distinction between two related but little used words: admonition and excommunication. *Admonition* is a gentle, loving yet firm reproof offered in counseling. It is a warning against a sin or fault. *Excommunication* is the process by which a member of the body is placed under an exclusion from the fellowship.

"My left arm? Oh, I discovered a hangnail, so naturally I had it removed."

Both of these ideas make us feel uncomfortable. Nevertheless, Jesus clearly teaches both of these actions in Matthew 18, and in a progression of moving from admonition to excommunication. Since He teaches both, we must take both seriously. It is a cancerous testimony for any group's witness before God and the campus when they see a brother or sister's sin and do nothing about it. On the other hand, the group is hurt by too hasty of an excommunication, for then the Christian community comes to be regarded as concerned not with restoration of its members to God, but for its self-image.

The initial approach in the disciplining act, whether it is called admonition, exhortation, rebuke, reproof, or correction, is a re-presentation of the gospel. This is to be done in a sincere and tender appeal. "If a man is overtaken in any trespass, you who are spiritual should restore him in a spirit of gentleness," writes the apostle Paul in Galatians 6:1

"Admonition of a sinner in the church is analogous to evangelism outside the church. As in evangelism repentance issues in forgiveness and fellowship, so in discipline response to the word of admonition issues in forgiveness and continued fellowship. Likewise, as in evangelism an individual's rejection of the gospel is respected and he is not incorporated into the body of Christ, so in discipline an individual's rejection of the word of admonition is respected and he is excluded from the body of Christ. The only difference is that admonition begins with a sinner in the church, whereas evangelism begins with one outside the church." Marlin Jeschke, *Discipling the Brother,* Herald Press 1972.

The goal is a sincere confession of sin. This is the obvious goal of the Matthew 18 instruction. This confession of sin brings renewed fellowship between the sinner and God the Father. Turning from the sinful life must follow, and repentance leads to renewed fellowship in the body of Christ.

The Qualifications To Execute Discipline:
"You Who Are Spiritual..."

Who are the "spiritual"? Let's look at Galatians 5. In verses 18-25, Paul tells believers to "walk", "live" and "be led" by the Spirit. Paul expects to see right actions flowing from right thinking.

How does one become "spiritual"? In verses 24 and 25, Paul adds, "Those who belong to Christ Jesus have crucified the sinful nature with its passions and desires. Since we live by the Spirit, let us keep in step with the Spirit." A spiritual person is one who seeks to kill sin in their life. They hate sin and its effects in their life. Beyond this, the spiritual man evidences the fruit of the Spirit. (Gal. 5:22, 23) This fruit appears as right attitudes or dispositions, and as manifestations flowing from us as from the Spirit.

It is very important to remember the "spiritual man" is a condition made possible by the person and work of Jesus Christ, not by any actions of a person alone. "For it is by grace you have been saved, through faith – and this not from yourselves, it is the gift of God – not by works, so that no one can boast." (Ephesians 2:8-9) Nonetheless, since you then are spiritual due to God's grace, you are the one, having seen the trespass, to go to your brother and gently, but resolutely restore him to the Lord.

The Healing in Discipline: "Restore Such A One"

"Restore" is a word used for executing a repair or for the work of a surgeon in removing some growth or setting a broken limb. We are to "restore" someone who repents. True repentance is evidenced by Godly sorrow. It is more than saying "I'm sorry." Godly sorrow produces good things in our lives. Paul explains this to the Corinthians, "For you became sorrowful as God intended.... Godly sorrow brings repentance that leads to salvation and leaves no regret, but worldly sorrow brings death. See what this godly sorrow has produced in you: *what earnestness, what eagerness to clear yourselves, what indignation, what alarm, what longing, what concern, what readiness to see justice done*" (2 Corinthians 7:9b-11a; italics added).

I propose the following guidelines:

- Restore someone who repents.
- Discipline someone who does not repent.

First Step of Discipline: "Watch yourself, or you also may be tempted."

"But watch yourself, or you also may be tempted" (Galatians 6:1b). Start with yourself. Proceed in a spirit of gentleness. One day the great preacher D.L. Moody walked along a Chicago street and saw a drunk lying in the gutter. He turned to his friend and said, "There, but for the grace of God, go I." We start with careful self-examination and repentance before the Lord of our own temptations. We cannot gloat over the grace we have received. That completely misunderstands the work of grace in our life. With a renewed sense of our own position before Christ - a sinner saved by grace through faith - we are then to go to our brother.

One more very important thing: forgive your brother from your heart before you go. In the larger scriptural context of Jesus' words in Matthew 18, Jesus teaches us to rid ourselves of anything that would prevent us from entering the kingdom of heaven. Do radical "spiritual" surgery where necessary. Then He tells us the Good Shepherd goes after the lost one from the flock. He describes the joy of the Father when one lost sheep is returned. Moving on we come to our passage, "If your brother sins, go to him..." He then talks to us about prayer for the ones who wander off, and affirms when two or three agree on such a thing, it shall be done for them by their Father in Heaven.

However, Jesus saves the punch line for last. He tells a story of a servant who is forgiven an incredible debt, and who turns around and punishes someone who owes him a day's wage. Jesus says this unmerciful servant will be punished severely. Jesus last words speak volumes, "This is how my heavenly Father will treat each of you unless you forgive your brother from your heart" (Matthew 18:35).

Putting It All Together: How to Restore

A. Personal introspection

Evaluate your own life, and make sure you are "walking in the Spirit", i.e. keep on becoming "spiritual".

B. Distinguish between sins and differences

Make sure you are evaluating your wayward brother from a biblical perspective. Be sure what you are confronting is sin and not a matter of conscience. Refer to the "Deeds of the Flesh" as a beginning guideline.

C. Pray

Confess your need of Christ's forgiveness; praise Him for His abundant grace in your life; pray that you will not be led into temptation; ask for guidance.

D. Forgive

Forgive your brother from your heart. Be merciful.

E. Meet personally

When sheep go astray.

Go to the wayward brother and discuss the area of concern. If it is in fact true he has fallen into sin, then ask for confession of this sin and further ask to see a turning from the sin. Do so in a spirit of gentleness, while at the same time not backing down from the truth of God's word.

F. Maintain confidentiality

Keep the circle of awareness as small as possible. Don't tell everybody about your brother's sin or even about you going to him. The goal is to "win" your brother back, and allow him to reestablish fellowship with the body of Christ. If the repentant person wishes to testify about his return to the Lord, let that be for him to choose. Unless, of course, the nature of the sin caused direct injury to the local Christian fellowship group, or it was a spiritual leader who sinned. Elders/leaders are to be disciplined publicly, but still with mercy. 1 Timothy 5:19, 20

G. Include a witness(es)

If your brother does not repent, then go again with one or two others. Again ask for a turning from sin and a turning to the Lord.

H. Include leadership

If still no Godly response, then approach the group's leadership and have them meet with the brother. If the brother persists in his sin, then decide with the leadership how best to present this issue before the body.

I. Keep restoration as the goal

Remember, the purpose of discipline is to win a brother and not primarily to maintain a pure community. The issue of corporate purity comes after the issue of personal purity has been pursued to the fullest.

J. Celebrate restoration

Jesus tells a parable where a shepherd leaves the flock of 99 sheep to go out after one lost sheep in order that the lost sheep might be restored to the fold. Immediately following this parable is a parable of a woman who looses one coin and searches until she finds it. When the lost coin is found she calls all the neighbors and has a party! Finally Jesus tells one last story about lost things - the parable of the lost son. When the son returns home to his father the reconciliation is celebrated. (Luke 14.1-32) It is good for you to find a way to celebrate with your friend who has been "won" back to God's love and grace.

K. Finally, do not fear personal failure.

The fear of failure takes the focus off the injured person and puts it on you instead. We live by faith, and this will certainly cause your faith to grow. Most importantly, eternity is at stake for your wayward friend.

Lesson 12

The Qualities of an Effective Discipler

Ready to Disciple?

So now you're ready to be a small group discipler. Or are you? How does one assess his or her own preparedness? By what gauge may a person evaluate whether to take a step of faith and assume leadership? Anyone who takes seriously the Lord's commission to "disciple the nations" will ask these kinds of questions.

In this lesson, I look at two grids or gauges by which you may self-evaluate. They come from my practical experience in campus ministry and then from Thessalonians.

Essentials for a Small Group Discipler

A. Godly Character

The most incredible news the world has ever heard: God came to earth! He provides a wonderful salvation, and makes Himself known to us. No more distant voices from a mountain or earthquakes or even still small voices, but God became a man. In doing so, He demonstrates the relationship He wants with us. He knew the most effective way we may come to know how to live, act, think, and love, is seeing a model. Not only are we to follow Him, but we are to become like Him.

This means our character needs to become conformed to His. Godly character qualities need to find a home in our lives such as the Beatitudes (Matthew 5:2-12), Fruit of the Spirit (Galatians 5:22-26), and the Rules for Holy Living (Colossians 3:12-17). These qualities are not taught, but caught.

A Bible teacher may explain them, but each individual believer must respond personally to the Lord to implement them into his or her life. To become like our Lord, a person must spend time with Him. Sharp edges must be chipped and polished, wild branches must be pruned. This interaction with the Lord is sometimes painful, but everyone who submits to this process will find peace and fruitfulness flowing from their life.

There are two reasons why a person's growth in Godly character is an important indicator for effective discipleship. First, those being discipled need a real example of who Jesus is. We aspire to say as Paul did: "Follow my example, as I follow the example of Christ" (1 Corinthians 11:1).

Second, those who are growing in Godly character are obviously in vital communication with Him. They are learning how to listen to God's voice and obey. They are submitting to God's discipline and are being developed by it. This process cannot be taught in, exhorted in, preached in, or even encouraged in; it is only invited in. The person in this kind of relationship with the Lord should be discipling others.

B. Pastoral Heart

The word "pastor" comes from the same root word for "shepherd". To care for people as a pastor is thus to care as a shepherd tends sheep. When the apostle Peter described a shepherd's heart, he underscores the motivation for leadership. A discipler leads because he or she is willing, not forced, eager not greedy, and serving not lording over. They desire to serve as an example to the flock. I Peter 5:1 -4

A discipler's heart breaks at the point of another person's need. They mourn with those who mourn and rejoice with those who rejoice. (Romans 12:15) They hate to see the damage done by sin and misfortune in a friend's life. Insensitivity in the hands of a spiritual leader is horribly destructive. A critical attitude will only compound wounds in a young believer's life. An effective discipler exhibits the warmth of Christ.

C. Vision

Life without vision is a dead-end. Jesus' first words to his new disciples were "Come and follow me," and "I will make you fishers of men." Vision is important in three areas:

1. Vision for Self

"It's high time you gave some thought to your future son. There's an Ice Age coming, you know."

A discipler sees God's direction through prayer and serious study of Scripture. He prays for direction to live by. A discipler is going somewhere, and is filled with hope for the future. The picture of a more preferred future captures him.

2. Vision for Individuals

A discipler prayerfully develops an image of a younger believer's growth and development in the Lord, as well as, how the members of the small group may grow as the Spirit of God is free to operate.

3. Vision for the Campus Ministry

The discipler desires to share the same vision for ministry that the corporate leadership feels called to fulfill. Vision is characteristically something shared between believers. It is a corporate issue.

D. Dedicated to God

A discipler is a Christian from head to toe. To be an effective discipler he must be totally sold out for God. He believes Jesus Christ is the only answer. It is a great temptation in today's society to be a humanistic Christian. However, it is not sufficient merely to help people to feel better. We will only truly feel better about ourselves when we are completely assured from within our sins are forgiven. It is not enough for people to have Christian friends and not feel lonely. Loneliness is only dealt with when believers walk in the light together. A Christian is not merely a moral person. A

Christian is a transformed person, a new creature (2 Corinthians 5:17). A Christian is an alien and stranger in this world, but is a full citizen of God's kingdom (Ephesians 2:19). A discipler understands this and is fully dedicated to God.

E. Ministry skills

An effective discipler has skills. A discipler knows the *methods* of discipleship as well as the *message* of discipleship. A discipler knows how to:

- lead a person to Christ
- facilitate worship
- lead a discussion
- form a group
- encourage people to share from their heart
- restore a brother who has fallen
- teach others how to pray
- assess another person's needs, and
- create a plan to minister to those needs

Wow! That's a lot! There is good news here though! Of these five essentials, the first four (character, heart, vision, and dedication) occur in a person who is faithful to God, and for that reason they are the most important. *All ministry skills may be learned.* Any person who is sold out for God may be taught how to be effective for the Lord. These skills come to us as a learned process.

The Apostle Paul Demonstrates Effective Discipleship

The second grid comes from the apostle Paul and his relationship with his disciples in the city of Thessalonica. The following are nine essential components evidenced in his interaction with this church.

A. An effective discipler is earnest in prayer.

"We always thank God for you all and always mention you in our prayers. For we remember before our God and Father how you put your faith into practice, how your love made you work so hard, and how your hope in our Lord Jesus Christ is firm.... Day and night we ask him with all our heart to let us see you personally and supply what is needed in your faith." 1 Thessalonians 1:2-3; 3:10-11

The effective discipler places complete reliance on a Power and Presence beyond him. Effective disciplers see themselves as being able to change the course of human events through prayer. They know any human activity apart from prayer is doomed to failure. Therefore, they intercede for those being discipled, ever offering them up to the Father who can "supply what is lacking in (their) faith."

B. An effective discipler is a proclaimer of the gospel.

"And there is another reason why we always give thanks to God. When we brought you God's message, you heard it and accepted it, not as man's message but as God's message, which indeed it is." 2:13

Effective disciplers believe completely in the power of the gospel to change lives. They are not ashamed of the gospel. (Romans 1:16) They proclaim the good news of Jesus because they know it will transform someone. Central to the task of discipling is telling others about Jesus and His love and plans for them.

C. An effective discipler is pure in heart.

"Instead we always speak as God wants us to, because he has judged us worthy to be entrusted with the Good News. We do not try to please men, but to please God, who tests our motives. You know very well that we did not come to you with flattering talk, nor did we use words to cover up greed-God is our witness! We did not try to get praise from anyone, either from you or from others." 2:4-6

The proper motivation for an effective discipler is to ever and always please the Lord and not merely please others. The discipler's heart is free from self-interest and the need to manipulate others. Integrity between what a discipler says and does is essential.

D. An effective discipler is an example of Christ-likeness.

"For we brought the Good News to you, not with words only, but also with power and the Holy Spirit, and with complete conviction of its truth. You know how we lived when we were with you;

it was for your own good. You imitated us and the Lord; and even though you suffered much, you received the message with the joy that comes from the Holy Spirit.... You are our witnesses, and so is God, that our conduct toward you who believe was pure, right, and without fault." 1:5,6; 2:10

"Hey Darrell! Don't you think you're taking this idea of making our lives open for inspection a bit too far?"

The lives of effective disciplers are open for inspection. They are people who are open and honest, letting the sincerity of their walk with Christ become observable. They testify as Paul said elsewhere, "Follow me as I follow Christ" (I Cor. 11:1). A discipler is a person who lives above reproach.

E. An effective discipler is a lover and nurturer of people.

"As apostles of Christ we could have made demands on you. But we were gentle when we were with you, like a mother taking care of her children. Because of our love for you we were ready to share with you not only the Good News from God but even our own lives. You were so dear to us! Surely you remember, our brothers, how we worked and toiled! We worked day and night so that we would not be any trouble to you as we preached to you the Good News.... As for us, brothers, when we were separated from you for a little while - not in our thoughts of course, but only in body - how we missed you and how hard we tried to see you again! We wanted to return to you. I myself tried to go back more than once, but Satan would not let us." 2:7-9; 2:17, 18

There is intensity in a discipler's caring and concern underscoring his ministry to others. Paul likened it to the tenderness with which a mother nurtures her child. Patient compassion is essential to building the love of God in someone. A discipler allows the fruit of the Spirit to express itself toward those he serves.

F. An effective discipler is an admonisher.

"You know that we treated each one of you just as a father treats his own children. We encouraged you, we comforted you, and we kept urging you to live the kind of life that pleases God, who calls you to share in his own Kingdom and glory." 2:11,12

Love demonstrates the strength to confront a brother or sister in trouble. To admonish is the necessary counter-balance to the previous quality of being a lover/nurturer. To admonish is our reflection of God's love, expressed in Hebrews 12:5-12, where every son is loved and disciplined. If disciplers fail to admonish, they are bound to reproduce disciples who are self-centered and unable to endure the hardships of life.

G. An effective discipler is a teacher and encourager.

"Day and night we ask him with all our heart to let us see you personally and supply what is needed in your faith. May our God and Father himself and our Lord Jesus prepare the way for us to come to you! May the Lord make your love for one another and for all people grow more and more and become as great as our love for you. In this way he will strengthen you, and you will be perfect and holy in the presence of our God and Father when our Lord Jesus comes with all who belong to him." 3:10-13

This demands a consistent study of the Scriptures. If disciplers are to encourage growth in someone else, then they must be continually growing themselves. Disciplers work at being effective at communicating this knowledge to others. Simple faith is essential, but stupid faith on the part of a discipler is an affront to the person of God and His people. Truth shared in love never fails.

H. An effective discipler is persevering.

"You know how we had already been mistreated and insulted in Philippi before we came to you in Thessalonica. And even though there was much opposition, our God gave us courage to tell you the Good News that comes from him." 2:2

The effective discipler is willing to go against the grain of his culture, being willing to become a prophetic person. Discipleship is emotionally taxing and time-consuming, thus demanding an ability to persevere. This quality is a direct result of prayerfulness and realistic biblical planning. If we are to help build lasting communities for Christ, then excellence in craftsmanship is required. This means a discipler must dig in and stick to a task with perseverance.

I. An effective discipler is open to receive personal ministry.

"... while we sent Timothy, our brother who works with us for God in preaching the Good News about Christ. We sent him to strengthen you and help your faith.... Now Timothy has come back, and he has brought us the welcome news about your faith and love. He has told us that you always think well of us and that you want to see us just as much as we want to see you. So, in all our trouble and suffering we have been encouraged about you, brothers. It was your faith that encouraged us, because now we really live if you stand firm in your life in union with the Lord. Now we can give thanks to our God for you. We thank him for the joy we have in his presence because of you.... Pray also for us brothers.":2, 6-9; 5:25

Effective discipleship is not a one-way street. Leaders will not produce other healthy leaders if they do not let others minister to them. If you desire humble, honest, confessional disciples, then be one. Beware of isolation, it breeds hostility, haughtiness and heresy.

Conclusion

After looking at these two gauges, how did your self-evaluation turn out? If you're like most folks on the planet, you will find several areas where growth is needed. Don't walk away because you realize God is not finished with you yet. Find a trusted leader and share your self-evaluation with him/her, and then agree to pursue the specific needed growth in Jesus.

Remember, it is God's will for us to disciple the nations. It is His idea. And since it is His idea, He is the One who equips us to fulfill His will. He delights in doing so. "For we are God's workmanship, created in Christ Jesus to do good works, which God prepared in advance for us to do" (Ephesians 2:10). "Being confident of this, that he who began a good work in you will carry it on to completion until the day of Christ Jesus" (Philippians 1:6).

Appendix 1

The Philosophy of Ministry For Chi Alpha Christian Fellowship

What is Chi Alpha?

Chi Alpha is a national organization of students in higher education who unite to express the person and claims of Jesus Christ to their campus communities and call others into relationship with Him.

Why does Chi Alpha exist?

Chi Alpha exists to participate in the fulfillment of Christ's Great Commission on campus. Chi Alpha takes its name from *christou apostoloi*, "Christ's sent ones". We find our identity and task in Paul's words, "We are therefore Christ's ambassadors...we implore you on Christ's behalf: Be reconciled to God" (2 Corinthians 5:20).

What does Chi Alpha seek to be in order to do this?

As ministers of reconciliation, we are a community of some of God's college-age people: a community of worship, a community of prayer, a community of fellowship, a community of discipleship, and a community of mission. We include the concept of "community" in all these because of the high priority we put on coming together as a group for biblically commanded activity. We will use the phrase "gathered people of God on campus" to stress our position that we can be more visible and effective as a group than as isolated individuals.

Community of ***WORSHIP***

By "community of worship" we mean that as gathered people of God on campus, Chi Alpha must first establish ministry to God as the highest call of Christians. They must embody the following principle:

a. we were created by and are now reconciled to God to bring glory to Him (Isaiah 43:7; Ephesians 1:11,12);
b. the family of Christ is the dwelling place of God for the very purposes of ministry to Him as His priests, and for proclamation of His greatness to the world (Ephesians 1:10-22; I Peter 2:4-10);
c. the presence of God is made real among men when Christians worship (Psalm 22:3).

Second, Chi Alpha expresses ministry to God by:

a. directing adoration to His person in giving thanks for his acts of loving-kindness toward us in all ways possible (Psalm 100; 150);
b. learning with Mary to sit at His feet and listen and respond to Him (Luke 10:38-42; John 10:4,5);
c. allowing the *charismata* listed in 1 Corinthians 12 to flow through us to the Lord; and
d. learning to worship Him in our actions (1 Corinthians 10:31; Hebrews 13:15,16).

Third, the community of worship expects other ministries to grow best when nurtured in an atmosphere of ministry to the Lord.

Community of ***PRAYER***

By "community of prayer" we mean: As a gathered people of God on campus, Chi Alpha must establish intimacy with God as the highest privilege of Christians. We recognize the importance of confession, affirming the lordship of Christ, the fatherhood of God, and the conviction by the Spirit (Philippians 2:9-11; John 16:8). We acknowledge to God sins that make us ineffective in our spiritual walk and pray for each other for forgiveness and restoration (Hebrews 12:1; James 5:13-16; Psalm 139:23-24).

In supplication we acknowledge God as our source and supplier (Philippians 4:6,7,19). We bring our requests to God, expecting Him to fully supply our needs. We look to God for daily guidance, open to His revelation.

In spiritual warfare we recognize we are spiritual beings in a battle that calls for spiritual weaponry (Ephesians 6:10-18). Prayer is a priority in breaking the strongholds on our campuses and in our society.

Through intercessory prayer we profess that God is the powerful healer and worker of miracles. We pray in faith that the sick may be restored. We stand in the gap praying His will may be accomplished on earth (1 Timothy 2:1; Ezekiel 22:30-31).

Community of ***FELLOWSHIP***

By "community of fellowship" we mean that as a gathered people of God on campus, we are in joint submission to Jesus' command, "As I have loved you, so you must love one another" (John 13:34).

The permanent motivation to pursue fellowship is the command of Jesus to love one another. The permanent pattern of fellowship is the example of Jesus' relationship with His disciples.

"This is how we know what love is: Jesus Christ laid down his life for us. And we ought to lay down our lives for our brothers" (1 John 3:16). By this we also know that the believer cannot live in isolation, but as a member of the body of the elect, joined together by the common life-source of the Holy Spirit. Because members of the body are priests and servants, they follow Christ's example of self-sacrifice on behalf of one another. This entails assessing one another's needs and responding with intercessory prayer and deeds of caring – "Rejoice with those who rejoice: mourn with those who mourn" (Romans 12:15).

This flow of love is enabled and sustained by the Holy Spirit and His gifts (1 Corinthians 12; Romans 12; Ephesians 4). It produces harmony among the members that reflects the relationships within the Triune Godhead, testifies to the divinity of Jesus, and validates that community's claim to be disciples of Jesus.

Community of ***DISCIPLESHIP***

By "community of discipleship" we mean that as a gathered people of God on campus we are committed to pursue the fulfilling of the Great Commission given by the Lord Jesus Christ, to "disciple" all nations (Matthew 28:20). Our discipleship finds its directive in the authority of God's revelation, the Holy Scriptures. We are the people of the Book. "All Scripture is God-breathed and is useful for teaching in righteousness, correcting and training in righteousness, so that the man of God may be thoroughly equipped for every good work" (2 Timothy 3:16,17).

It is our conviction that discipling is best accomplished in the relational context of the matured believer helping to nurture younger members of the community in small group situations, even as Jesus discipled the Twelve, and as the disciples went from house to house. By this process each member is thus given the basic knowledge and skills necessary to grow toward maturity in Christ and is equipped for the work of the ministry (Ephesians 4:11-16).

We desire to follow the instructions of Paul and Timothy, "The things you have heard me say in the presence of many witnesses entrust to reliable men who will also be qualified to teach others" (2 Timothy 2:2). In this way we perpetuate a continuous development of maturing leaders for the work of Christ in a collegiate community.

Community of ***MISSION***

By "community of mission" we mean: as gathered people of God on campus, Chi Alpha is committed to the task of completing the mission of Jesus – to make disciples of all nations (Matthew 28:19) and "to seek and to save that which is lost" (Luke 19:10). We commit to seeing every circumstance in every location as an opportunity to share the gospel in word and deed, empowered by the Holy Spirit.

We believe that the mission of Jesus is at the core of what it means to be the people of God. Immediately prior to his return to heaven, Jesus commissioned us, his followers, as the primary agency for taking the message of reconciliation to every nation (Matthew 28:19; Mark 16:15; Luke 24:47; John 20:21; Acts 1:8). We are obliged to give every person a clear presentation of the gospel, and must be committed to this task as individuals, in our local chapters and as a national movement.

A Christ-like lifestyle must also accompany our proclamation of the gospel. John's gospel records that Jesus told us "Your love for one another will prove to the world that you are my disciples" (John 13:35, NLT). Our love and care for one another, coupled with acts of love and service to our communities and world demonstrate the truth of our proclamation and the reality of God's love to those who are not yet believers. What we do, as much as what we say, makes the gospel attractive to those we are seeking to reach (Titus 2:10).

Our mission must also extend beyond our local campuses and communities to reach the entire world. God has given us a tremendous opportunity to fulfill this mission by bringing international students from around the world to study on our campuses. By befriending, loving, proclaiming the gospel to international students and connecting them to the indigenous body of Christ before they return home, we will impact the world (as Phillip did with the Ethiopian eunuch, Acts 8:35-39).

Finally, each student in Chi Alpha should recognize the unique purpose God has for their lives, and to heed the call to live their lives intentionally for Christ (2 Corinthians 5:14; Ephesians 2:10). We encourage each student to be active in fulfilling this mission beginning on their own campuses and living as Christ's ambassadors in the world at large. While God will call some to vocational ministry and missions, every student in Chi Alpha can impact the world through intercessory prayer, sacrificial giving and living as a disciple of Jesus Christ and his representative in the world. We place a priority on preparing students to live the mission of Christ as a primary lifestyle by connecting them to the local church to be strategic and deliberate in their involvement in the campus, the marketplace and the world.

Our Strategy

Our primary strategy is to work toward the building of a group or community of people who share these ideals. We believe the most fertile atmosphere for people to come to faith and maturity in Christ is warm exposure to a group of people fervently committed to the God of the Bible, to one another, and to the task of evangelizing the campus. As a worshiping, loving, discipling, witnessing community, they demonstrate the kingdom of God and most effectively enculturate others in it.

Appendix 2

Discipleship Small Group Leader Job Description

Purpose

A. As a community of discipleship, we are committed to pursue the fulfilling of the Great Commission given by Jesus Christ, to disciple all nations (Matthew 28:20).

B. It is our conviction that discipleship is best accomplished in the relational context of the matured believer helping to nurture younger members of the community in small group situations, even as Jesus discipled the Twelve and as the disciples went from house to house.

C. We desire to follow the instructions of Paul to Timothy, "The things you have head me say in the presence of many witness entrust to reliable men who will also be qualifies to teach others" (2 Timothy 2:2). In this way we perpetuate a continuous development of maturing leaders for the work of Christ in a collegiate community.

D. Thus, a Small Group Leader (SGL) is the primary leader who accomplishes the fulfilling of the Great Commission on campus. A SGL is a student trained and set apart to disciple fellow students in the context of a small core of students within the Chi Alpha ministry.

Responsibilities

A. A SGL is to be active in follow-up of new student contacts for the purpose of the formation of a discipleship small group.

B. A SGL is to build a sense of community among the members of his/her small group, and to see each member tie into the larger Chi Alpha ministry on campus.

C. A SGL is to do 1-to-1 discipleship with the committed members of his/her small group in the following areas:

   1. Spiritual development – nurture relationship with God; foster Godly morals, choices, and lifestyle; protect new disciple from influences that could destroy faith in God.
   2. Compassionate heart – minister to others at their point of need and train them to do the same.
   3. Vision – foster faith to believe God to work dynamically in the disciple's life and cause the disciple to develop a clear sense of God's call on his life.
   4. Zeal – foster a total commitment to God in every area of his life.
   5. Ministry skills – train the disciple in areas of spiritual gifts, disciplines, and capabilities.
   6. Truth – direct the disciple in building a solid doctrinal foundation.

D. A SGL is to make the Bible the textbook for all discipleship.

E. A SGL is to focus on leadership development in the members of the small group.

F. A SGL is to foster an awareness of and participation in mission among the small group members.

G. A SGL is to provide compassionate discipline and correction, keeping all matters in strictest confidence.

H. A SGL is to foster worship, personal sharing, and prayer in the small group meeting beyond the content study.

Requirements

A. The following is a list of deeds and character qualities that should reflect the SGL. They are to be compassionate for those in need. They lead voluntarily and with eagerness, not lording over others, but examples to the small group members. They are people of prayer and humility, above reproach to those in the Chi Alpha group, and have a good reputation to those in the world. They are sensible, able to encourage with sound doctrine, not addicted to any controlling substance, and gentle. And finally they are not be a new convert.

B. Small Group Leaders shall be accountable to fellow Small Group Leaders and to the campus ministry staff.
C. A SGL must have been a member of a small group for at least one semester.
D. A SGL must be trained in discipleship as offered by the campus ministry staff.
E. A SGL must be willing to serve a one-year commitment running concurrent with the academic calendar.
F. A SGL must interview each Spring to serve as a SGL for the next school year.

Commitments

A. Attend the main weekly meeting of Chi Alpha.
B. Lead their small group weekly meeting.
C. Adequately prepare for their small group meeting.
D. Attend regular meetings for the Small Group Leaders.
E. Participate fully in the life of the Chi Alpha ministry
F. Attend a local church.
G. Have a regular 1-to-1 session with each member of the small group.

Appendix 3

Small Group Leader Interview

Name.....................
Date.......................

A. ***Basic Information:***

- How long have you been in Chi Alpha?
- How much longer will you be in college?
- Have you read and understood the Small Group Job Description? Are you willing to follow these guidelines?

B. ***Commitment to Christ:***

- How long have you been a Christian?
- Please describe your personal devotional life. What does it look like?

C. ***Commitment to Biblical Relationships:***

- Are there people to whom you are accountable for how you are living your life as a Christian? Who are they? Are you giving those relationships a high priority?
- Are you allowing others to get to know you, to know your strengths and weaknesses and receive their help?

D. ***Commitment to the World:***

- What is your view of evangelism?
- How does personal evangelism find expression in your life?

E. ***Commitment to Leadership?***

- What skills do you possess that enable you to serve with effectiveness as a Small Group Leader?
- What liabilities would you bring to this capacity? How would you compensate for these?
- What priority would Small Group Leadership receive from you?
- What motivations do you have for being a Small Group Leader?

F. ***Commitment to God's People:***

- Describe the vision you have regarding Chi Alpha on this campus?

G. ***Commitment to Godly Character:***

- What evidences may you point to that demonstrates you're a faithful person?
- Are you a person of self-control? in your personal finances? in your time management? patience in accomplishing tasks?
- Is there anyone you are aware of that would object to you serving in a small group leadership capacity? Are you blameless before others?

H. ***Commitment to a Spirit-filled Life:***

- What do you believe the Bible teaches on the ministry of the Holy Spirit in the individual's life?
- What evidence of the Holy Spirit do you see in your own life?

Appendix 4

Resource Leader Job Description

I. Title

Resource leaders are those affirmed by Chi Alpha to serve in the following areas:

A. Supervision of specific small groups and their small group leaders, in order to maintain and foster spiritual oversight, loving relationships, leadership development, and mission.
B. On-going development of small group leaders.

II. Responsibilities

A. Provide prayerful spiritual assessment of small groups within Chi Alpha.
B. Develop the small group's long-and-short term discipleship goals.
C. Serve the pastoral needs of small group leaders.
D. Provide compassionate discipline and correction, keeping all matters in strictest confidence.
E. Assist with the appointment of small group leaders.
F. Help to promote outreach to the campus through the small groups.

III. Requirements.

A. Character qualities of resource leaders: compassionate toward those in need, lead voluntarily, eager, not lording over others, person of prayer and humility, above reproach, a good reputation, sensible, encourage with sound doctrine, not addicted to any controlling substance, and gentle.

B. Resource Leaders are accountable to the Staff.

C. Demonstrate confidentiality and personal integrity.

D. Specific Requirements

1. Actively involved in Chi Alpha for one year.
2. Effectively lead a small group for one year.
3. Willing to serve a 1-year commitment.

IV. Commitments:

A. Attend main weekly meeting.

B. Participate fully in Chi Alpha's programs.

C. Attend a local church.

D. Attend a regular resource group meeting composed of resource leaders and staff.

E. Assist in coordination of the small group leaders meetings.

F. Attend an annual planning retreat.

G. Conduct biweekly 1-to-1 meetings with small group leaders.

H. Aid in coordination of new student follow-up.

V. Scriptural Foundations

The following scriptures are seen as foundations for resource leadership: Matthew 20:26b-28; Acts 20:28-35; Ephesians 4:11-16; 1 Peter 5:1-3. These passages highlight the role of pastoral oversight in the church. We do not see resource leaders to be elders, however we do desire they pattern their heart and life after the example of biblical elders.

Appendix 5
A Small Group Covenant: Key Ingredients for a Healthy Small Group

The commitment of affirmation:

There is nothing you have done or will do that will keep me from loving you. I may not agree with you actions, but I will love you as a person created and loved by God, and I will support you with God's affirming love.

The commitment of availability:

What I have is at your disposal if you need it, to the limit of my resources. As part of this availability, I pledge my time, whether in prayer or in a mutually agreed upon meeting time.

The commitment of prayer:

I commit to pray for you regularly, believing that our caring Father wishes his children to pray for one another and ask Him for the answers they need.

The commitment of openness:

I strive to become a more open person, disclosing my feelings, struggles, joys, and hurts to you as well as I am able. I will trust you with my stressors and my dreams. This is to affirm your worth to me as a person.

The commitment of honesty:

I will try to mirror back to you what I am hearing you say. I will express this in love and honesty in a controlled manner.

The commitment of sensitivity:

I desire to be known and understood by you. I commit to be sensitive to you and to your needs to the best of my ability. I will try to hear and draw you out.

The commitment of confidentiality:

I promise to keep whatever is shared within the confines of the small group, in order to provide the atmosphere necessary for openness.

The commitment of accountability:

I am accountable to you to become what God has designed me to be as His loving creation.

We the undersigned know we are not everything listed above, but we pledge to each other to try our best to become these things to each other through this small group.

Signed: ____

Appendix 6

How to Facilitate Sharing in a Small Group

1. Model what you want the other members to do.

Your example determines the character of your group. If the tone you set is defensive, suspicious, and shallow, you'll have a defensive, shallow group. On the other hand if you model vulnerability and affirmation, your group will follow your example. Don't expect others to do what you fail to demonstrate by example.

2. Deal with experience before ideas.

Theoretical discussions kill in-depth sharing. This includes doctrinal discussions. It is possible to play intellectual ping-pong, bouncing ideas off each other without ever going any deeper than the conceptual level. But when we share what we know to be true through experience we share ourselves, and in doing so we share all Christ means to us. Before you tell what you think and believe, show what you feel, who you are, and what you know to be true from walking with Christ.

3. Deal with the here and now.

The past is interesting, and at times it is valuable to share it, but the focus of a small group meeting should be kept on what is happening now. Rehearsing your past can be superficial chitchat. There are exceptions, of course, such as when you share something you experienced that made a significant impact and contributed to who you are today.

4. Don't disrupt.

Listen carefully to each person as they share. If the individual is sharing something really important to them, it might mean the agenda for the evening adjusts to let them share what is on their heart. This does not apply to someone who dominates a discussion with shallow conversation.

5. Don't explore.

Encourage people to share what he or she wants to, but don't make him or her share what they do not want to. If someone in the group starts to probe, say something like, "Let's let Jill tell it the way she sees it." or "Why don't we give Jill a chance to finish what she has to say?"

6. Don't give directions.

Advice is cheap and sometimes disastrous. If someone in the group has had a comparable experience to another's situation, allow them to share the experience, but do not go on to draw the conclusion for the person. If the person specifically asks for advice, tell what you might do if you were in their place.

7. Don't criticize.

When someone shares a sin or failing, the group will face a crucial test. The person should not be put down. If he or she is, they will possibly never open up again. The group should accept them as they are. Only to the extent the group accepts the person for who they are will they be able to make a really lasting change in their life.

Appendix 7

A Guide to Resolving Small Group Problems

If a Group Member Creates a Problem

1. *Member won't participate.*
   Involve them in conversation. Find out about their personal interests. Devote some time to him or her outside the meeting. When they do take part, make a special note of it. "That's a good point, Joe. We haven't been hearing enough from you. We appreciate hearing your position." Use questions to draw them out. Ask direct questions only they can answer. Don't use a question that can be answered "yes" or "no" or ask a question he or she might be unable to answer.
2. *Member is joker, life of the party.*
   Encourage this when tensions need released. Laugh and enjoy it. However, when it is time to move on and tensions are relieved, ignore the efforts at frivolity. The person will soon learn their role is the productive release of tensions, not to waste time laughing it up when the group should be discussing.
3. *Member monopolizes discussion.*
   a. Encourage this if he or she is contending for a role that benefits the group the most. If not, interrupt the person and move

to another member. In general, encourage the group to take care of folks like this.

b. Don't embarrass or be sarcastic. You will need this person in this role later. Do not let them monopolize or give long speeches. Interrupt politely and throw the ball to another member with a question. "Good point Ted, now Bill what do you think?"

4. *Member is argumentative, obstinate*

   a. Keep your temper. Don't let the group get too tense and excited. Antagonism breeds further antagonism. Remember, the group is partly responsible for the individual's behavior. What can the group do to change it?

   b. Examine the member's position carefully. Find merit in it if possible. Do not close your mind to the ideas just because they are expressed in an opinionated way. The group must examine all sides. In an emergency, let them know time is limited and you will be glad to talk to him or her later. Talk to the individual privately before the next meeting. Explain that his or her view is important, the group will consider it, but it must not destroy group effectiveness.

If the Group Creates a Problem

1. *Group is lost, confused, doesn't want to go to work. They ask directions, complain they have been wasting time. Feel the discussion lacks organization. Members say they want to do something.*

   Now is the time to suggest a way of working. Provide agendas and suggestions for systematic ways to go about discussion. If you are too forceful, it will be resisted or rejected. If you provide structure now, it will be welcomed.

2. *Group is tired, apathetic, dull. Marked lack of interest, low response rate, tired, yawning, quiet, polite.*

   Small talk, joshing, kidding, humor. Make them smile, chuckle, laugh. Display as much enthusiasm and energy as you can. Keep pumping enthusiasm until it is caught. Maybe play the devil's advocate.

3. *Group is resistant, antagonistic, hostile. Members argue, come in conflict, show personal antagonism.*
   Assess the most useful role for each person. Agree and support members who assume suitable roles. Joke, use humor, change the subject. Remind the group of its objectives. If necessary, face situations and bring role struggles into open-talk about the social interactions.
4. *Group is enthusiastic, responsive, active. Members stimulate one another to ideas, enthusiastic agreement, everyone interested and involved.*
   Go with the flow of the group. Allow the group to be democratic in direction and leadership. Do not worry too much about sticking to the planned agenda. Right now exploit the group's creativity.

Appendix 8

PROAPT

Date:_______________

Pray	***P**urpose: Here I am Lord…just as I am* ***R**elax: I have this time and I give it to You* ***A**sk: Come to me Lord…by Your Spirit* ***Y**es: I believe this time will be ordered by You*
Read	*Read closely, out loud, and slowly* *(1 to 3 times)* Today's Passage:___________________
Observe	*Observe what the text says* *(copy/arrange/outline/interact with the text)* *(Now stop and simply spend some time in quiet thought, then…)*

Apply	I think the direction from the Lord today to me is…
Pray	***A****doration: I love You Lord* ***C****onfession: Forgive me Lord* ***T****hanksgiving: I thank You Lord* ***S****upplication: I ask You Lord*
Tell	*I will pass on what I heard from the Lord to someone else.* *What:* *To Whom:* *How/when:*

Adapted from Discipling Ministries Seminar, Barnabus, Inc. Used by permission, 1991.

Appendix 9

PROAPT: A Sample

Date: *September 17*

Pray	***P**urpose: Here I am Lord…just as I am* ***R**elax: I have this time and I give it to You* ***A**sk: Come to me Lord…by Your Spirit* ***Y**es: I believe this time will be ordered by You*
Read	*Read closely, out loud, and slowly* *(1 to 3 times)* Today's Passage: *1 Thess. 4:9-12*
Observe	*Observe what the text says* *(copy/arrange/outline/interact with the text)* *"brotherly love" – Paul seems to say, "You're doing good at this but do even more."* *"God-taught" – Seems Paul coined this word. In Isa. 53 one of the evidences of the new age of salvation is the youth are taught by God. Paul is implying the new age of salvation is now happening.* *"make it your ambition to lead a quiet life" (NIV)* *"make it your ambition to have no ambition"* *(Phillips Bible)*

	"seek restlessly to be still" "be ambitious to be still This sounds like Paul is using an oxymoron here (like 'friendly fire" or "Lone Ranger Christian") *Paul encourages them to:* *1) abound in brotherly love more and more* *2) aspire to live quietly* *3) tend to their own affairs* *4) work with their own hands* *(Now stop and simply spend some time in quiet thought, then...)*
Apply	I think the direction from the Lord today to me is... *Paul gave the Thessalonians an "A" in brotherly love. He'd probably give me a "C" in Brotherly Love 101* *They had problems with being busybodies. I am the opposite. I am more like a hermit.* *They were obsessively concerned with the end-times. I don't have enough end-time expectation.*
Pray	*Adoration: I love You Lord* *Confession: Forgive me Lord* *Thanksgiving: I thank You Lord* *Supplication: I ask You Lord*
Tell	*I will pass on what I heard from the Lord to someone else.* *What:* To show brotherly love I will invite Tom to eat lunch next week *To Whom:* Tom *How/when:* I'll talk to him after class today.

Adapted from Discipling Ministries Seminar, Barnabus, Inc. Used by permission, 1991.

About the Author

Raised in a Christian home Harvey A. Herman entered secular university student ministry in 1973 immediately following his graduation from Evangel University. He and his wife Sally pioneered and directed five Chi Alpha Christian Fellowship groups in Iowa, Missouri, and Nebraska. He served as senior pastor of a university church in Seattle, and coordinated staff training on the national leadership team for Chi Alpha for most of the 1990s. Presently, Harv is the area director for Chi Alpha over the American Northeast.

Along the way he earned a masters in biblical studies and later a doctorate in strategic leadership and organizational management from Regent University.

His daughter Sarah married a Scot named Rob. She is a campus pastor at the University of Aberdeen, Aberdeen, Scotland. His son Matthew married his college sweetheart, and they direct the Chi Alpha campus ministry at Cornell University.

Sally first experienced university ministry as a senior in college. After a time in the Army nurse corps she re-engaged in student ministry and introduced it to Harv. For over three decades they have been partners in student ministry. Sally most recently directed Chi Alpha at Georgetown University School of Medicine.

You may contact Harv at HarvXA@hotmail.com or visit the website: harvsallyherman.net

CPSIA information can be obtained
at www.ICGtesting.com
Printed in the USA
JSHW052148250521
15189JS00001B/3

9 781606 476444